The Truth about Prodigals

Words of Counsel to Parents and Friends

The Truth about Prodigals

Words of Counsel to Parents and Friends

Will Simmons

Copyright © 2016 Will Simmons

All rights reserved. No part of this book may be reproduced, scanned, or distributed in any printed or electronic form without permission.

First Edition: 2016

ISBN: 978-0-9988812-6-3

Unless indicated otherwise, Scripture quotations are taken from the
New American Standard Bible®,
Copyright © 1960, 1962, 1963, 1968, 1971, 1972, 1973,
1975, 1977, 1995 by The Lockman Foundation
Used by permission.

Great Writing Publications

Taylors, South Carolina

Dedication

This book is dedicated to the staff and professors in the Biblical Counseling Department at the Master's College, for their faithfulness in delivering God's principles found in the Word of God to all the issues we humans face, even amongst a world filled with psychological descriptions, empty solutions, and hollow hopes. They continue to swim upstream against this tide, delivering trust and hope that brings lasting healing to heart issues.

Appreciation

Will Simmons has done a good job addressing such an important issue in the realm of biblical counseling.
Here is a resource that counselors can use regularly as a tool in their ministries; I hope it receives a wide readership.

Dr. John Street, Professor and Chair of the graduate program in biblical counseling, The Master's College and Seminary, California

Chapter Contents

Foreword: Rick Holland 13

A Testimony from Friends 15

Preface: A Message to Family and Friends of a Prodigal 19

1. What Is a Prodigal? 27

2. How to Identify a Prodigal 33

3. Why Prodigals Live As They Do 45

4. How Not to Respond to Prodigals 55

5. How to Treat a Prodigal 69

6. Coming to Grips with the Truth about Your Prodigal 81

7. Whose Fault Is It? 93

8. The Real Issue: Jesus as Master 111

Postscript: Closing Words to the Hurting 127

Foreword
Rick Holland

The expectations of parents for a newborn are unmatched. Will my son grow up to be a godly leader? An entrepreneur? A pastor? The President of the United States? Will my daughter develop into a sweet woman who can serve the church? Be a helpmeet to her husband? Lead others by her godly example? Be a model of purity? Every Christian parent has the highest hopes and dreams for that little bundle of joy.

But something happens only a few months after the bubble gum cigars and "Welcome Home Baby" balloons. No matter how good the parenting techniques, no matter how godly the parents, no matter how much the environment is controlled, every child's sinful nature begins to express itself. No parent ever had to teach a toddler how to disobey. It comes all too naturally.

The goal of Christian parenting, then, is to administer gospel truth that will glorify God, bring joy to our children, and mitigate the effects of the Fall. However, very possibly, something happens to some of our little ones. As they grow and mature, there is a painful stiff-arm thrust in the face of parents. There is a rebellion against God and His standards. Out of nowhere, it seems the story of the prodigal son is not just a Sunday school lesson; it is being played out in high definition before our eyes.

Foreword

I have worked with parents and their children in pastoral ministries for almost three decades. The stories of parents who have lost their grip on a prodigal child (or two or more) are heartbreaking. But the accounts of those same parents who have lost their grip on God are even worse. It seems that a new book on Christian parenting comes out almost weekly. But sadly, there seems to be little real help for dealing with a problem child, a prodigal.

That is why I am so thankful to see Will Simmons' book published. There are various people it can serve: a loving friend to parents of a rebellious child; pastors and leaders who want to equip their flock to handle such heartbreaks; and, most importantly, parents looking for help with a wayward son or daughter. This is not just a "how to" book. It is a biblical, theological treatment of handling a prodigal in your family. I have every confidence it will not only give you parental wisdom; it will make you love the gospel more. In fact, you will no doubt begin to translate the lessons about waywardness to your own relationship with God.

Don't open these pages without a strong spiritual stomach. It is good medicine, but very potent. I believe you will find encouragement, hope, counsel, correction, but, most importantly, God. Enjoy this journey into a new level of spiritual maturity!

Rick Holland, founder of the Resolved Conference, author of Uneclipsing the Son, a regular teacher at The Master's Seminary and The Expositor's Seminar, and pastor of Mission Road Bible Church, Prairie Village, KS

A Testimony from Friends

A Testimony from Friends

Almost a quarter of a century ago, in the perfect sovereignty of God, my wife, Sherli, and I adopted our third precious child into our family. The first two had been adopted at birth and picked up from the hospital as newborns. Our third child, our Prodigal, was already over two years old when we first met him. A pastor of a church had been asked to help place this little boy, who had been born out of wedlock to a fifteen-year-old mother. He had suffered emotional trauma at the hands of his family, who no longer wanted the responsibility of caring for him. Our Prodigal was finally adopted into our family shortly after turning three. He came to us with many problems: hate, anger, unwillingness to submit to any kind of authority—caused by the intersection of his sinful nature with the adversities of his formerly tumultuous environment. In our naiveté, Sherli and I thought that a few months in a loving Christian home would transform him into a normal little boy. We were very wrong.

Our Prodigal was defiant in his attitude, even to the point of being violent toward other children when they crossed him. He habitually lied, stole, would not listen or obey, and was lazy. As he grew up, he only became more hardened and bolder in carrying out his sin. We sought counseling, read books, and talked to friends. We did everything we could think of, but our precious son had no heart for any of it. He had no care for how his behavior was affecting his siblings and our home. Things got so bad that we had to send him to boarding school as a young teenager. This was the most emotionally painful thing my wife and I have ever had to do. When he was old enough he joined the Marine Corps only to be kicked out for repeated involvement with drugs. Once he was out of the Marine Corps and on his own, he was free to live his life with no restraints. His life sadly became more

A Testimony from Friends

debauched, resulting in four separate occasions of incarceration.

All along, we have prayed fervently for him, sought to make available to him every kind of help, in the church and out, but he has never had a heart for any of it. In his own words, our Prodigal said, "I just don't care." He was raised in a Christian home where God's Word was taught on a daily basis. He attended a strong Christian church where pastors, leaders, and family friends regularly extended themselves to him. He was loved and people cared about him, but none of this could make our precious son love God or want to obey Him. He stated that he didn't want our lifestyle and that he was not comfortable at church.

We feel like the Apostle Paul in 2 Corinthians 4:8-9: "We are afflicted in every way, but not crushed; perplexed, but not despairing; persecuted, but not forsaken; struck down, but not destroyed" as we wait for God "who works all things after the counsel of His will" (Ephesians 1:11). Shortly after we adopted our Prodigal, we changed his middle name to Paul, in the hopes that one who was "formerly a blasphemer and a persecutor and a violent aggressor" (1 Timothy 1:13) would someday like Paul embrace "the faith and love which are found in Christ Jesus" (1 Timothy 1:14).

The Bible's message is highly relevant to prodigals. Read and consider what Will Simmons has to say as he draws lines of application from the Scriptures to the challenging circumstances that people face in our modern world.

Rufus and Sherli Harvey
(Rufus is the CFO of Grace to You.)

Preface

A Message to Family and Friends of the Prodigal

Preface

"Look, I know all about God; I spent all my life in church and I'm sick of it. Just leave me alone and let me live my own life."

These words may sound familiar. Many a parent or friend has heard them from those who have become prodigals. Perhaps as parents, we raised them with the best we could give them, with what we knew as parents at the time. Perfect? Probably not, but still with love. Then there comes the black sheep who goes astray, out into the world with all its sinful influences, promising fun and thrills, only to leave one battered, embittered, and broken. Perhaps, as a parent, you may have failed to discipline your child in biblical ways, much like David had with his son Adonijah in 1 Kings 1:6. He was the fourth son of David. He rebelled against David and sought to take over his father's throne. Within this context nestles a little verse that's very revealing. It reads, *"His father had never crossed him at any time."* David loved his son, but a lack of proper discipline created a son of rebellion, irresponsibility, and eventual death.

You may now be starting to face the consequences of this in your own life as a parent or friend. As your children grow into adulthood, beyond your responsibility, they unwittingly wander into a debauched lifestyle that leaves them dependent on either the state or on others around them, following a lifestyle totally foreign to how they were taught. Jesus talked about a father whose youngest son did this very thing. He was called "the prodigal." The Greek term means "dissolute." It was not merely wasteful extravagance, but there was also much immorality (Luke 15:11-31). It conveys the idea of an utterly debauched lifestyle. Such is the end of a prodigal. Sin never blesses, and people do not improve with its prevalence in their lives. Yet, as we will see later on in the book, this affliction is sometimes the very thing God uses to bring about repentance, often stripping prodigals of their evil desires for worldly things and turning them to God. This is much like what the prodigal went through in Luke 15:17f:

But when he came to his senses, he said, "How many of my father's hired servants have more than enough bread, but I am dying here with hunger. I will get up and go to my father, and say to him, 'Father, I have sinned against heaven and in your sight. I am not worthy to be called your son; make me as one of your hired men.'"

As a parent or friend of a prodigal, you may perhaps have already experienced many heartaches, stressful situations, financial loss or emotional pains. Let me give you an example. It's a true story of one such family I had counseled at my church.

These people were church members and had one son whom I'll call Bob. He grew up in church but when he reached the age of seventeen, he decided he had other interests, and church wasn't one of them. This shattered the parents' hopes for their son, and they watched as he slowly developed friendships with people who were into parties, drugs, drinking, and immorality. As the years passed, and Bob moved out on his own, one problem after the next arose. There were unpaid tickets, there was no money to pay the rent, no food, and all this along with a list that would go on from month to month. Sad stories, excuses, guilt trips and mostly lies poured out of Bob; but these stories were ever so convincing to his parents. Bob's life was what the Book of Proverbs talks about.

He will die for lack of instruction, and in the greatness of his folly he will go astray. (Proverbs 5:23)

Preface

Parents may expose their children to the gospel, but if it's not in their hearts to accept it and follow God's principles as adults, they will choose the world's ways. Even though a child may be exposed to the truth many times for many years, the grace of God is not bestowed upon anyone just through being in a Christian environment. It only comes through His grace when there is sincere repentance from sin and a heart that yeans to follow Christ. The destructive nature of Bob's blindness in sin can lead anyone, as it were, to walk alongside death. In the Book of Proverbs, death is portrayed as a gradual descent with many problems. Trouble, financial difficulties, broken relationships, and many more afflictions follow them as these growing young adults move away from God and the love of their parents.

In our story above, the leaders in the church tried to help the parents in dealing with Bob, endeavoring to give them some objective perspectives on the young man's lifestyle of irresponsibility and sin. But the parental love and care they had once shown for their little child continued to be lavished over their young adult, as they tried to save him from harm. Not realizing it, these parents were handicapping Bob from facing the consequences of his lifestyles of sin and sinful choices. Proverbs gives believers some sound advice on these matters.

He who withholds his rod[1] hates his son,
But he who loves him disciplines him diligently.
(Proverbs 13:24)

Exercising biblical discipline involves much more than administering mere spankings; it is being consistent in verbal

---

[1] (Withholding the rod refers to failing to exercise discipline.)

Preface

disciplining and then following through with what you've said. It is living out a righteous lifestyle that is filled with consistency in all areas of the parents' lives, showing the child an example of obedience to Christ and His word and a true love for God and His people. But, parents who fail to be consistent in disciplining their child in the adolescent years are practically showing a hatred for their child by not directing that young adult toward a righteous lifestyle. Parents often fail to do this because of laziness, distractions due to entertainment, a fear of loss of love from their child, or a preoccupation with their own lifestyles. This seems to be prevalent today in many Christian households. As these children become adults like Bob and live lives filled with irresponsibility, do the parents need to show godly discipline if they really love them?

So many times I've seen parents of adult children strive (all in the realm of parental love) to play the role of the Holy Spirit, unknowingly by trying to convert them, trying to save their souls. They seem not to realize that this is a supernatural act of the Spirit of God. False assumption of a child's salvation actually breeds false assurance in the prodigal's heart as that young person thinks that he can have heaven and have his sin.

In our story, Bob's parents failed to heed the counsel of their pastors. As time went on, they kept saving Bob from his troubles, all at the expense of their own financial wellbeing. Eventually Bob became an alcoholic and ended up in jail. When his mother came to bail him out, the chaplain took her aside and talked to her about the need to leave Bob alone and let him face the consequences of his own actions.

But she wouldn't listen, and bailed him out again from jail. By this time Bob was thirty years old and had left behind a trail of emotional and financial hardships for his parents.

This kind of story is common with parents, especially those

Preface

whose adult child is on the streets, leading a lifestyle that's filled with habitual sin and with little care about God, sin or the parents hurt. After all, who would really want to take such a person in? I do realize from personal experience that there are varying degrees of prodigals, and this in itself must cause anyone to use wise discernment in dealing with them. So what does God expect from family members or friends who have a prodigal in their midst?

As a parent or friend of someone who grew up in the church, you may be dismayed, wondering how anyone exposed to sound biblical truth could make such foolish choices. Your heart aches because you know the spiritual and physical consequences of those choices. Much like our story in Luke 16, when the son rebelled and wanted to leave and pursue a worldly lifestyle of sin, the father graciously and lovingly released him with his inheritance. The father illustrated here is God. I've learned, in my fifty-plus years as a Christian, that God graciously gives the prodigals what they want in their rebellion and uses those same things as a tool of affliction some time later to actually bring them to repentance. Why? All out of love—the love of the father who plans things in such a way as to bring the prodigal back into the fold.

A Case Study in Consequences: Bob

Bob was obviously a troubled person because of his habitually sinful lifestyle. Now he was facing the consequences of many of his wrong choices. When we look through the lens of the Bible's teaching, it is evident that Bob didn't have a chemical imbalance, he wasn't bi-polar, and he didn't need antidepressants. Rather, he had chosen to live in sin and now he was facing the consequences of those wrong choices. Sin is a reality, even if the world has chosen to jettison the term "sin." We live in a moral universe with a moral God who has warned us time and again that sin does exist and that it is inexhaustibly destructive. And because God is a moral being, He judges sin and He has designed that there will be repercussions for sin. However, His very nature of care and love could not allow us to be so destroyed unless He acted, as He does.

That's why Bob had reached the situation he was in. It wasn't his parents' fault; neither was it society's fault; nor was it because of some childhood incident. Rather, it was Bob choosing to follow the desires of his sinful flesh, and he was now having to live out the consequences. But God was acting. He was not silent. In all this He was orchestrating things in such a way as to bring about His divine will.

When you look at how his life was working out in practice, Bob wasn't the only one facing problems. His family and friends were also greatly troubled because of his afflictions, as is usually the case in these kinds of situations. They suffered many hardships—financially, emotionally, along with guilt and stress—while trying to help Bob out of his sinful wallowing over the years.

One of my uncles in Louisiana had a few pigs on his dairy farm. One day as a young lad I was once helping him clean out the pig pen. Within minutes of our finishing the task, the pigs were back in the mud.

Each time Bob's parents tried to help, he would let them down, showing disrespect and ungratefulness, quickly leaving for several days without notice or, even worse, engaging in blatant sin in their home. And while he was acting this way, he was even gossiping about the very ones who were trying to help. They still tried to reach out to him—over and over again—from motives of love as well, at times, from false guilt.

Preface

Eventually family and friends reach the point where they become frustrated with people like Bob and they shut the door, many times themselves walking away in sinful behavior. So what is a person to do in cases like this? First, let's get a clear picture in practical terms of what a prodigal really is. We know that each case is different for each situation. However, we must all be overshadowed with motives of compassion and love, yet at the same time exercise wise discernment in the decisions we make.

1

What Is a Prodigal?

What Is a Prodigal?

It has been said that love is blind. How true this is! It can be devastating when someone goes astray, especially when that person is a family member or close friend. Perhaps that person has been brought up in a Christian home and at church. It brings hurt, rejection and dismay.

Maybe you have a close friend who has been brought up with high moral values, and all of sudden there that person is, out in the streets, choosing to live a life of destruction. And because that person is so close to you, your love for him or her blinds you from being objective, causing you to lose the ability to use wise biblical discernment in your relationship.

As will be discussed later on in the book, sometimes unwise things are done towards prodigals—such as giving them money, repeatedly bailing them out of jail, or letting them move in to your home, even though they are perhaps disrespectful or deceitful or have no heart to change.

This happened to someone within our family. She was raised in a Christian environment but when she came to adulthood, she chose to live a life of sin. Many years later the repercussions of those choices brought her to a point where she was living alone, after three failed marriages, in an old motor home out in the streets. Eventually the vehicle broke down and we decided to let her move in with us. As soon as she came, dissension, arguments, and lies came into our home. She made it clear she wanted help but she wanted no accountability for her behavior, even though we gave her much freedom. After several months, she decided to move back out into the streets. And as of today, she is still causing dissensions within different families who have tried to help her.

But the question has to be asked: What is a real prodigal? Is such a person still a Christian? Was this individual ever a Christian? These and many more are discussed later but the

What Is a Prodigal?

real issue here is defining what a real prodigal is!

So let's start from the beginning. The dictionary defines a prodigal as *"a person who spends, or has spent, his or her money or substance with wasteful extravagance; spendthrift"*[2]

The actual word is morally neutral, and can be placed in a context of good or bad. In Luke's Gospel, the terms *squandered* and *loose* place this word *zao* (the basic meaning of the word *zao* is *to live*) in a negative way. The term *prodigal* comes from the phrase in Luke 15:13 *"And there he squandered his estate with loose living."* Loose-*living* in the original Greek language is *"zao"*—*to live quickly*. The actual word translated in English as *prodigal* is not used in the text, but the meaning clearly shines though in the story. It is a picture of a sinful son, throwing aside what he knows to be right, choosing instead to follow his feelings of the flesh, leading him towards affliction. It pictures a person raised in a religious home, but lost. Sadly, this is the course many people follow.

On watching a series on TV, I learned of a reporter who was compiling an undercover story with the police in catching pedophiles. In almost every case, when caught, the criminals said they knew in their hearts that what they were doing was wrong, but they followed their sinful desires. That is the way it is with most people. God has placed within us all a conscience, a warning beacon, telling us what is wrong and right, and a homing beacon, telling us to whom we should head—that is, toward the Lord our Creator, the Father, a loving, merciful God. This is clear from the following passage:

...in that they show the work of the Law written in their

---

[2] http://dictionary.reference.com/browse/prodigal

> *hearts, their conscience bearing witness and their thoughts alternately accusing or else defending them. (Romans 2:15)*

And what does it take to turn this person around from a sinful lifestyle? Goodness, graciousness, truth? No, it often takes affliction! The prodigal in Jesus' story would not think of returning to his loving father until he had lived out his inheritance. He never thought about repenting until he had to eat with the pigs and had hit bottom. Humans are usually very hardhearted toward change if they are fulfilling the desires of their sinful hearts, and usually it is not until affliction and trouble come their way that they are willing to seek God. This is why it is the wise person, in this life, who follows the Lord and His word instead of yielding to the sinful pulls of the flesh (and thus avoiding afflictions arising from a sinful lifestyle).

The story in Luke is about two lost sons; both were raised in a godly home with a father who loved and served the Lord. The underlying principle illustrates two kinds of people. The first is the prodigal who is devastated by sin's destructive consequences but comes to God truly repentant. The other son is a picture of Israel's religious leaders who thought that they were the example of godliness and humility when in, reality, they were the opposite.

In contrast, this prodigal is an example of the person who turns away from an initial exposure to faith in Christ. He chooses instead to live a life of sin, then only to hit bottom and come to true repentance towards God, and so is made willing to do anything to find forgiveness, mercy, love and guidance. *"But when he came to his senses"* is the point of Luke 15:17. The father in this story represents God, gracious and wise, and His unending love to reach out to those who come repentant to Him.

So, if the term prodigal in Luke 15 pictures a lost person, what does a true believer look like? It is only as we have a clear picture of characteristics of a saved person that we can clearly identify the lost. I know it's hard sometimes to do that. When our loved ones go astray in sin, we desperately want to see any hint of salvation in them because we know God exists, and because we are concerned about the judgment that awaits all.

Being objective (and being objective is not to be coldhearted) in situations like this is necessary in order to pray, hope and trust God that the prodigal will come to true salvation. As we do this, it's important to start this journey by laying the correct foundation. We must develop a biblical perspective on both what a true Christian is, and understand the prodigal in order to recognize him and learn how to graciously and wisely minister to him. And it will be through this biblical lens that we not only judge ourselves, but also the prodigal. We must first recognize that Jesus is our Master and we are His slaves. We'll be looking at this later on in the book.

2

How to Identify a Prodigal

How to Identify a Prodigal

This is probably the hardest thing to do, especially for those close to a prodigal. Because we love and care for the person, it is possible for us to develop a blindness at this point. To objectively look at the decisions and lifestyles of our adult children is very often difficult because of the emotional attachment we have with them. It tends to either blind us to the harsh truth of their sin, or it has the effect of massaging the truth of the situation to the point that we, as parents, compromise our own core values. This eventually causes more hurt to ourselves, relatives, friends and their adult prodigals.

Some of the safeguards to these things include the following:
- being trained in the Scriptures and living by them on a day-to-day basis;
- judging and discerning according to biblical principles helps us in evaluating how to deal daily with our prodigals;
- being in a local body of believers where the Word of God is taught clearly, accurately and in an expository way, which is so helpful when it comes to gaining biblical principles to live by;
- being connected to pastoral leadership for counsel in situations like this. These pastors can help us look objectively at the situation of our adult prodigal's situation and can properly come alongside us in dealing with them in love yet having discernment, and lastly,
- being able to measure our love for God. Jesus said in Matthew 10:37 that our love for Him should supersede any kind of familial love.

Functionally, many times parents say they love God, but then there comes a point when their own adult children get in the way. Now they must choose between the two. At this point, God is relegated to a back seat. Values and priorities are set aside and, instead, some kind of emotional defense mechanism kicks in so things are said and done that were once condemned in others. It is at such a point that the true measure of the parents' love for God becomes evident and is found to be no better than that of a heathen.

BE ON YOUR GUARD!

So, how do you prevent this from happening? Let me give you a few pointers I've learned in over thirty years of counseling in dealing with prodigals;

- As a parent, evaluate your faith, trust and real love for God by looking at your own life. Is it basically self centered?
- Always (and honestly) develop the ability to check your real motives for why you do things. It will be quite revealing! Most people rarely delve into why they do things or say things. It can be a most rewarding adventure if you are able to realize the truth about yourself and what your real motives are for doing certain things in your life.
- Undertake a Bible study on the word "love" in the New Testament.
- Talk to your spouse about what Jesus means when He says, "Follow Me." What does that really mean in biblical terms?

In dealing with prodigals, how could we spot one in, for example, a home or church setting? Prodigals regularly go to such places where there are unsuspecting prospects for money, food or a place to stay. There are some common characteristics that are noticeable for these kinds of people.

For myself, being a parent has given me the experiences I needed to learn some of these valuable lessons, and many years of ministry in the security department at my church has exposed me to a large number of prodigals. Dealing with them has not only helped me understand how they think, but has given me the ministry tools necessary to help. Here are some of the principles I've learned over the years about prodigals in the local church.

Resisting Counsel and Discipline

When confronted with their sin or sins, even with an attitude of love and grace, anger is the common response. When confronted, they tend to disappear; only to re-appear in a different home or church, spreading gossip about how *"mean"* the others had been toward them. They want help, but they want no accountability or counsel. They are, at this point, living a self-centered lifestyle, and they have no real intention to change.

UNTRUSTWORTHY

They usually make many promises, tell sad stories about their lives, and can even sound very convincing, but deception becomes a common thread. Because of this practice, they become very good at this sin of deceit, even deceiving the most discerning.

The Importance of Submission

This is the obvious pattern of their lives. They are lost and walking in the flesh, so the fruit of their lives will be a pattern of rebellion. In dealing with them, realize where their heart is towards God: in rebellion. The litmus test here is not only the sharing of God's principles, but seeing over time if they are serious about applying these principles to their lives. In most cases, they are not willing to submit to God or to your counsel. Don't be surprised.

How to Identify a Prodigal

In Love with Sin?

This may hurt you, but it's true. Satan is their father and they will act like him in various areas of their lives. Even if the prodigal is a family member—and in that we may think familial love for us will motivate him towards change—these family expectations may let you down. At this point the words of Jesus here must be kept in mind:

> *If anyone comes to Me, and does not hate his own father and mother and wife and children and brothers and sisters, yes, and even his own life, he cannot be My disciple.*
> *(Luke 14:26)*

Jesus set before us a principle that goes against our natural feelings of reluctance to act in a way that possibly could divide relationships—much like it did in His life. The only one who initially believed in Him was His own mother. It wasn't until after the resurrection that His own brothers and sisters believed in Him. (See Matthew 13:54-58, Mark 6:3-6, John 7:5, Acts 1:14 and 1 Corinthians 15:7.) They thought He had lost His mind. If we obediently do the right things, no matter how we feel, both protection and conviction can occur for the prodigal as well as those affected by the prodigal. Our love for God must be above and beyond that of both others and ourselves so that our desire to please the Lord Jesus Christ supersedes that of helping prodigals continue in their sin. To be a true disciple of Christ, our love for Him must be greater than all else, even the natural and ever pulling desire to love ourselves.

HUMILITY

Their unwillingness to submit to God, church leadership or to God's Word yields a lifestyle of rebellion, confusion, lack of direction and chaos. Therefore, don't expect real humility from them when it comes to loving us or the Lord. Again, realize deceitfulness may be a part of their lives, so they say, *"Sure,"* when the results will really be, *"No, I won't."* Pride and self centeredness is at the heart of their being prodigals in the first place. Humbling themselves before the Lord would only mean dethroning themselves, and this they will not do at this point in their lives. Be patient, pray, showing love and continue to focus on Christ.

Self-reliance
Because they are walking in the flesh, they make many foolish decisions, and this becomes a pattern in their lives. If anyone gives in to this, they will only be a recipient of their bad decisions and any kind of biblical counsel will seem foreign to them.

WHEN THERE IS NO FEAR OF GOD

Many prodigals may even say they believe in God, and maybe they do. But, as I have said before, so do demons! It's one thing to believe God exists; it's a whole other thing to submit ourselves to Him. Prodigals refuse to submit to God by not submitting to His Word, church leadership, or their parents. Because their father is Satan, they will act like him and live a life of rebellion. The reality is simple; they really don't believe God exists—certainly not as He has revealed Himself in the Bible. Neither do they believe that any repercussions will occur to bring them to accountability. You don't fear what you don't believe is there!

Holiness and Righteousness
Most prodigals think in extremes. They will either see them-

selves as really good people, just misunderstood, or as really bad people. Because of either one of these, they don't care what others think of them. Their habitual lifestyle is usually filled with lies, deception, and schemes of how to get money, fame, sexual favors, pity or flattery, all with disreputable motives. At this point they are blinded to the truth and any spiritual realities.

When Tongues Are Wagging...

One of the common practices of prodigals is gossip. When one looks at the Bible, there are many words used in describing one who gossips. Terms such as babbler, a whisperer, slanderer, accuser, [one who] brings charges and busybodies are used. These words all describe the same kind of sin that most people have practiced many times.

There are several truths in Scripture about gossip that we can learn.

First, gossiping about others isn't necessarily about lies; the things spoken about someone could be true.

Second, gossip is a common characteristic of the prodigals.

Third, gossip is usually done behind other people's backs—that is, when they are not present. Some people think that if you're willing to speak to them face to face, then it won't be wrong. But it must be said here that even if you do tell them face to face, it will still be wrong because of your motives. The intent of gossip is crucial. When it comes to this area, we need to ask ourselves three questions:

- Is it my position or role to reveal information about other people?
- Do I really plan to help that person? Is that my motive?
- Would I tell that person what I am saying now, with sincere motives? Is it truly out of love?

Fourth, many times a gossip discusses things that are even improper to talk about. This may include sexual or personal details of a person that it is not right for anyone to mention.

Fifth, if a person has a habit of gossiping, it could disqualify him or her from any kind of leadership within the church, such as being a teacher. Instead, one ends up being a very poor witness, not only to the lost but a very poor testimony as a Christian.

Sixth, the Bible teaches that if a person does gossip, he or she is prying into the private affairs of others (1 Timothy 3:11). Usually gossip is done between two or more people and what usually happens is very destructive to another person's character, testimony and relationship to others.

Seventh, the Bible also teaches in the Book of Romans that God gave those up to depraved minds because they rejected Him; one of their characteristics is gossip.

He who goes about as a slanderer reveals secrets,
Therefore do not associate with a gossip.
(Proverbs 20:19)

The Hebrew word for gossip here is *"pathah"* and is a word that means *to be spacious, wide open.* This is referring to the mouth that is wide open to spread this sin of gossip to others.

For I am afraid that perhaps when I come I may find you to be not what I wish and may be found by you to be not what you wish; that perhaps there will be strife, jealousy, angry tempers, disputes, slanders, gossip, arrogance, disturbances.
(2 Corinthians 12:20)

How to Identify a Prodigal

The Greek word for gossip here *is "psithurismos"* and is translated whisperer/gossiper. Paul the Apostle had planted the church in the city of Corinth. There was much wickedness in this city; it was filled with wicked people, and one of the evil things they did habitually was gossip. After becoming Christians and accepting Christ as their Lord and Savior, they were still practicing this sin. This was something Paul says a true Christian should never have as part of his or her lifestyle. In the verse above, Paul uses the term *"backbiting."* It could be translated *"to speak against, to slander."* In contrast to gossip, which involves subtle, isolated, behind-the-scene activities, backbiting goes further in defamation, slandering, or outright vilification of that person, which all stems from arrogance and results in divisions, disturbances and hurt. In Romans 1:26-29, Paul is discussing gossip of unconverted people. He writes in this passage about the lost: *"For this reason God gave them over to degrading passions... being filled with all unrighteousness, wickedness, greed, evil; full of envy, murder, strife, deceit, malice; they are gossips..."* Do any of these things describe anything in your life?

1 Timothy 3:11 states that *"Women must likewise be dignified, not malicious gossips, but temperate, faithful in all things."* Here the apostle Paul is writing to his young disciple Timothy who is now the pastor of his own church. He uses the word *"likewise"* for a very good reason. He has just completed discussing the role of the deacons. *Likewise* means the deacons are not to be men who are gossips or slanderers. Again the Greek word Paul uses here for a slanderer is *"diabolos"* and is one of the names given for Satan, the chief slanderer himself. *Likewise,* Christian women should never be known as a gossip; instead they are to be dignified, not gossips. This Greek word *"diabolos"* has the idea of bringing *charges,* usually with hostile

intent. In the same letter (1 Timothy 5:13), Paul discusses how women should conduct themselves in the home and with other women. *"At the same time they also learn to be idle, as they go around from house to house; and not merely idle, but also gossips and busybodies, talking about things not proper to mention."* Here Paul is clearly laying out the attitude, motive and lifestyles of Christian women, making the point that it should be one in which gossip is never a part of their lives. Such people speak nonsense, talk idly, make empty charges, and even accuse other people with malicious words. These kinds of people are very suitable targets for false teachers. The term *busybody* literally means *one who moves around*. The implication is that such people pry into things that should not concern them, and that they do not mind their own business. They are neither part of the solution and nor do they have the motive of encouraging and helping that person toward being more Christlike. Sinful words and actions will never lead to a person becoming more like Christ, only like Satan!

> *But realize this, that in the last days difficult times will come. For men will be lovers of self, lovers of money, boastful, arrogant, revilers, disobedient to parents, ungrateful, unholy, unloving, irreconcilable, malicious gossips, without self-control, brutal, haters of good, treacherous, reckless, conceited, lovers of pleasure rather than lovers of God, holding to a form of godliness, although they have denied its power; Avoid such men as these. (2 Timothy 3:3-5)*

These are powerful words written by the Apostle Paul to his disciple Timothy. He is describing not only people of his own time but how things will be during the last days before Christ comes back. They will be gossipers, and he's describing non-

Christians. Why is this so unusual? In God's ways, no true Christian lives a life of gossiping. If they tell anybody anything, it is for the other person's encouragement, for building up and for the pursuit of holiness. Paul says, in this verse, that these kinds of people have *a form of godliness*. What this means is they are religious and may even call themselves Christians, but the fruit of their lives shows they're really not, and one of those fruits is gossip, much as in the case of our prodigals.

He who goes about as a talebearer reveals secrets,
But he who is trustworthy conceals a matter.
(Proverbs 11:13)

Here is the opposite of what the Scriptures are describing above. A talebearer is one who gossips, slanders or destroys with words in contrast to the silence of the wise. A talebearer depicts someone who is a peddler in scandal, who speaks words deliberately intended to harm others. A trustworthy person conceals matters that might be injurious to others, while those walking in sin reveal secrets to others and are therefore not trustworthy.

What is the real motive of the prodigal for talking about others? Is it because he is seeking the improvement of his own welfare and has a sincere interest in his own wellbeing? In all the years I've been a Christian, there has only been a handful of times where I have actually been with people who were discussing the lives of others and it was very obvious they had their best interests at heart. You could see that they had a sincere love and care for this person and their words and choice of words showed that. Not so for the prodigals. So beware, and do not be surprised when you hear of them gossiping about the very ones who tried to help.

3

Why Prodigals Live as They Do

**LESSONS FROM THE BIBLE:
AARON AND HIS SONS**

Why Prodigals Live as They Do

There is a true story told about Aaron's two sons and a scenario that cost them their lives. It is found in Leviticus 9:22-10:3. It is the account of how children can be raised within the realm of religion yet where they decide to do what they want, eventually having to face the ugly consequences of their actions. It provides an example of how parents should respond when their adult children face the consequences of their sins.

These two sons—Nadab and Abihu—had become so familiar with God that they felt they could live as they pleased and act irreligiously as they felt. God had become unholy in their eyes, and their behavior showed this. Nadab and Abihu were two men who took their ministry in this nonchalant manner. Their father was Aaron and their uncle was none other than Moses. Among all the young men in the tribes they had such a privileged upbringing. They had firsthand accounts of what God had done with Moses. They were ordained to the priesthood in Leviticus 8:30. They actually shared in the encounters with God as they, too, were called up to the mountain with Moses and their father, as recorded in Exodus 24:1-2. They got to watch the supernatural phenomena occur. Verse 10 says *"they"* saw God and all His glory. Because of their heritage, and because of these personal encounters with God, today they may well be called *spiritual celebrities.*

In the passage in Leviticus 10, they had been preparing for several weeks with their father on how to perform their priestly service at the tabernacle. They had been given very specific instruction as to their duties. Then during this time of offering, they had seen, with their very own eyes, fire coming out from before the Lord and consuming the burnt offerings (9:24). And standing behind Aaron were these two men, next in line for the priesthood.

It's also interesting to note that after all these unique experiences, training and privileged work, here in Leviticus 10, they were stepping forward and starting their first official work as priests in the tabernacle. In what follows, we see several careless things these two men practiced that cost them their lives. Their lives provide examples for us of how children may be raised and taught about God but, when they become adults, go their own way into the world of sin and sensuality. They thought that because they believed in God, all was well. They thought they could live lives full of deceit, irresponsibility, rebellion, gossip and a host of habitual sins without having any accountability to a Holy God. They did not realize that God's wrath hung over their heads.

I would like to point out a few things Nadab and Abihu did that caused God to bring His judgment upon their lives. (Read Leviticus 9 and 10 for the full picture.)

Knowing Is Not Enough

Nadab and Abihu, in their own prodigal ways, decided to follow their own directions in life, thinking God would overlook their sinful hearts. This is very common with prodigals. Many prodigals devise a dual universe in which they can live as they do, thinking God is too caring to judge them for it or that He will have such pity upon their sorrowful lives as to not judge them. As we refer to the passage in Leviticus (see 9:24), we note God's presence in the Holy of Holies and how fire came forth to consume the offering. On seeing this, the reaction of the people was to shout and fall on their faces. It was worship and fear at this awesome event.

During one of these holy events, Nadab and Abihu rose and started doing things not even commanded by the Lord (10:1). In this scene, all the people were on their faces, but the two brothers rose, took some *"alien"* fire[3] and approached God, stepping into the Holy of Holies—the central part of the tabernacle—to worship Him on their own terms, even in their own intoxicated way. This is what most prodigals do. They live making feeling-based decisions while thinking perhaps they are actually Christians and that God will somehow, maybe out of pity for their afflictions, overlook their sinful lifestyles. Jesus made it very clear about the lifestyle of true believers. It should be one of obedience and a sincere pursuit for purity, all out of a genuine love for what God has done for us all. God is a God who both demands and deserves to be glorified. Certainly He should never be dishonored, disobeyed, and, even worse, sneered at as One who doesn't punish sin. As these two priests boldly enter the Holy of Holies with sinful hearts, the passage reveals God's reaction: *"And fire came out from the presence of the LORD and consumed them, and they died before the LORD"* (Leviticus 10:2).

Nadab and Abihu did several things that caused them to be struck down by the Lord. First, it appears they didn't take coals from the altar of incense. They brought some alien fire. This means they brought their own fire, showing disrespect and dishonor. It suggests that the fire that God had authorized was of little value to them personally.

It was also clear that only the high priest could enter the Holy of Holies. This was to be once year, to offer things to God. According to Leviticus 16:1-2, they tried to enter the Holy of Holies. They had been given no orders from Aaron or Moses to act this way.

And lastly, they were probably drunk when they did all this,

---

[3] The term "alien" fire is from Wycliffe.

showing a flagrant and unholy disregard for God (Leviticus 10:8-9). There is an important parallel between these two men and many prodigals—the point of verse 1: *doing things which God has not commanded them.* They acted on their own and thought God would pass it all by. So, if you expect a prodigal to act with common sense, to make decisions or to consistently act responsibly, you have wrong expectations. You are more likely to see a variety of responses such as irresponsibility, conflict, confusion, deceit, disobedience and a life filled with disorder. With anyone walking in the flesh sinfully, you can expect fleshly results.

Underestimating God

Certainly what these two men did caused God to bring judgment. When repercussions occur in prodigals' lives because of their sinful lifestyles, they may blame God or others for their afflictions, rather than blaming themselves. This is common for people in these situations. These two men in chapter 10 were acting both irreverently and hastily toward God's majesty and holiness, and God responded quickly. Fire came out and incinerated them both. Verse five records that their relatives carried them out still dressed in their tunics, which means that they were burnt from this lightning bolt from the inside-out, without their clothes even being burned. God's judgment was sure, right and quick. The verses also say they *died before the* LORD which means they were probably inside the Holy of Holies, by the Ark of God. Solomon writes about people like this in the Book of Ecclesiastes.

> *... follow the impulses of your heart and the desires of your eyes. Yet know that God will bring you to judgment for all these things. (Ecclesiastes 11:9)*

It is quite true we have a God who is extremely patient, merciful, and caring toward us, but it is also true He is a righteous judge and His judgments are fair. For prodigals, their afflictions are sent to bring them to repentance. Discipline and afflictions are as uniquely crafted as snowflakes are. But one thing prodigals do insistently is push the patience of God to unbiblical lengths, thinking God will not act. But God will act, and He is acting. They are not going through trouble because of natural causes; God is judging them, and they are suffering the repercussions of their sin. The Apostle Paul said:

For the wrath of God is revealed from heaven against all ungodliness and unrighteousness of men who suppress the truth in unrighteousness.
(Romans 1:18)

Prodigals actually see themselves as sometimes immune from the disciplines of God and, sad to say, trouble becomes so much a part of their lives that it becomes a norm.

Ignoring God
Moses spoke to Aaron after his two older had been cut down by God:

Then Moses said to Aaron, "It is what the LORD spoke, saying, 'By those who come near Me I will be treated as holy, And before all the people I will be honored.'" So Aaron, therefore, kept silent. (Leviticus 10:3)

These two sons of Aaron were guilty of violating both requirements of God's standards, and His standards have not changed. Exodus 19:22 is clear: *"Also let the priests who come near to the*

Why Prodigals Live as They Do

LORD *consecrate themselves, or else the* LORD *will break out against them..."* Has God lowered His standards to let prodigals have an excuse to go on sinning? Never! Even right now, they stand under the judgment of God. That is what you're seeing in their lives—trouble, hardship, afflictions, and for some, even death.

Nadab and Abihu offered strange fire, but that is not at the core of the issue here. Rather, it was their motives to begin with. This only goes to show that one can be semi-religious and lost. Prodigals may say they believe in God, but deep down inside their motive is for sinful desires that clearly outweigh any kind of love for God, which only goes on to make the point that if they refuse to love God, you should not think for a moment they will love you back either. These two men were very religious and acted religiously as priests to God, but God struck them down for violating His commands, for having nonchalant motives toward Him, and for showing an outright bad example to others.

AARON. . .

The key is found in verse 3 where we see Aaron's response. He had just witnessed his two drunken, disrespectful and proud boys go into the Holy of Holies and then die before his eyes. Was he mad, angry or complaining?

AARON HELD HIS PEACE

In spite of losing his two sons, he subjected himself to the righteous judgments of God. When parents have an adult child who is a prodigal, and their child refuses to repent and continues in a sinful lifestyle, parents or friends often let their own personal love for that prodigal supersede their love for God, and may even complain to God or the church leadership for both the consequences that are occurring in the prodigal's life or making the prodigal accountable for their behavior. The right response should be submission to the Lord and His ways, trusting in the very nature of God Himself—One who is extremely loving, merciful and patient, One who desires that all people come to know Him. It is at this point parents or friends need to step back and let the prodigal face the consequences of the choices that have been made.

I realize this isn't easy. It's a natural response for parents to help their children when they are in trouble, and rightly so if they are minor children. But when they come to the age where they are accountable, real heart issues come to light in their own lives. If these adult children choose to live a life of sin, even after knowing about God and His ways, a wise parent will relinquish them for a season to God. As Moses told Aaron after the death of his two sons, so he tells every parent, *"By those who come near Me I will be treated as holy, And before all the people I will be honored" (10:3)*. I must admit it is one thing for an adult child to live an immoral and irresponsible lifestyle, but it's even worse for those who have been raised and exposed to the gospel to turn their backs on God and actually treat Him as unholy, of little worth, without being willing to bring Him glory. The judgments of God will be greater for these than those not exposed.

When parents choose to ignore this and cater to their sinful and rebellious adult children's lifestyles by saving them each time, this, too, is an affront to God. Can you imagine for a moment if instead Aaron had became angry, walked up to the Holy of Holies, and told God that He was wrong in killing his two sons and that he, Aaron, could have changed them? God probably would have killed Aaron on the spot, too!

There is a common principle I teach my students at the Master's College, in my Biblical Counseling class. You should not take personal responsibility for the decisions of others. In the same way, parents cannot and should not take responsibility for their adult children's choices. If they lose their lives, those parents should realize that God is a righteous judge and that He never makes a mistake. The noteworthy thing about Aaron's response is he said nothing. He understood; he agreed. God is holy and He will not be mocked by those who want to treat Him, through their rebellious lifestyles, as unholy. He will act. If it is not today, it may be over the course of years of affliction in their lives. But realize this, that God's wrath is just not poured out on these particular kinds of sinful adult children, but it is also poured out upon everyone on earth who has chosen to not put his or her faith in God's Messiah: Jesus Christ.

"Who will not fear, O Lord, and glorify Your name?
For You alone are holy;
For all the nations will come and worship before You,
For Your righteous acts have been revealed."
(Revelation 15:4)

There is no one holy like the LORD,
Indeed, there is no one besides You,
Nor is there any rock like our God. (1 Samuel 2:2)

Who is like You among the gods, O LORD?
Who is like You, majestic in holiness,
Awesome in praises, working wonders?
(Exodus 15:11)

After the death of Aaron's two sons Nadab and Abihu, can you imagine the impact it had on Aaron's other two younger sons, Eleazar and Ithamar? After they had witnessed these events, they must have been profoundly impacted by them. They, too, would one day serve as priests before the Lord. And when you consider their ministries, they are seen to be much more honorable and consistent than those of their two elder brothers.

When God brings His righteous judgments upon those in rebellion, it has a wide impact on family and friends. It is here at events such as these that God is seen to be serious about His holiness and the things He has commanded.

4

How Not to Respond to Prodigals

**LESSONS FROM THE BIBLE:
ELI AND HIS TWO SONS**

How Not to Respond to Prodigals

Many parents raise children within a local church, hoping they will grow up following the Lord. But as experience teaches us, this is not always the case. Notwithstanding all their efforts, teachings and prayers, as soon as they are old enough, away they fly out of the home to pursue sinful lifestyles. It's as though they never had any exposure to Christ or the Bible at all. Many hopes and expectations are dashed to pieces as these adult children live as though God is of little value. It leaves parents shaking their heads in wonderment, asking the age-old question, *"Where did we go wrong?"*

This could be a valid question. We, as fallen creatures, are not perfect! Bad attitudes, misplaced values, selfishness, making our children idols (and many other such sins) can plague us all; yet the responsibility of those adult children eventually rests upon them and not on us. If they were to die and stand before God, He allows no finger-pointing. If one does not shelter under Christ as Lord and Savior while living here on earth, there will be no divine lawyer in heaven for one's defense—Jesus Christ, our Advocate or Defense Lawyer

All parents can do with these kinds of prodigals—these adult children—is to pray for them, while continuing to remind them of their exposure to truth, and then to wait with great, longsuffering patience. Sometimes we have to wait till they fall to their lowest point in affliction because of sin, and are willing to listen once again to God's word. Afflictions sometimes have to strip away the desires of this world so that the prodigal desires to seek the Lord. Many come to this point crippled in sin, often with deep wounds. But others reject Christ and never come to salvation. This can be a challenging time for parents or friends as they feel compelled to consider their own spiritual walk.

Experience has taught that even though there are always those few prodigals who finally turn, the majority of adult children never do. Year after year passes without a change. But through it all we, as parents or friends, learn more through the school of pain and hurt than we could learn from a book. Our theological understanding is tested, our prayer lives are deepened, and we are driven more to delve into God's Word to strengthen our faith and trust in the sovereignty of our Lord than ever before.

These same miserable prodigals that deal out hurt, emotional pains and agony to parents, friends and relatives are the very instruments used by God to sift the wheat from the chaff. This either proves the parents' own progress in sanctification, or exposes the false faith of those who were religious, but never truly saved to begin with.

But there is something worse than this. It is when there are parents who allow their children to wallow in sin, both in the home and within the church. I remember vividly one of many instances of this. A high school girl attending Sunday classes in our church caused many a boy to stumble into disobedience and sexual sins. Many times she would come with her parents to church, only to walk off campus with some boys, later to return just before church was over. When her parents were finally lovingly confronted about their daughter's behavior, they quickly became angry and defended her. In their view, the church leaders were wrong. They even accused them of lying and acting in racist ways. Eventually the parents left the church and joined another one. As time passed, the truth of their daughter's actions came to light with her pregnancy and riotous living. A living hell ensued as the parents tried to deal with their daughter.

As Christians, we should do our best to love, teach and exemplify to our children a Christlike lifestyle, but in all these things realizing that we must also trust in the discernment, discipline, and biblical teaching of the spiritual leaders within our local church.

And above all, our love for Christ must be above all else. Jesus had something to say about this: in Matthew 10:37:

He who loves father or mother more than Me is not worthy of Me; and he who loves son or daughter more than Me is not worthy of Me. (Matthew 10:37)

This brings us to our true and hopeless story of parents putting their children before the Lord. When you come to Christ, you must devote yourself fully to Him above all else. It's not that you can't love your children as any parent should; this is only natural. But what Jesus is emphasizing here is your ultimate devotion and your obedience to do what is right toward your children, young or adult, no matter what the consequences may be.

As part of a home school league, I can vividly remember many times when I would see how parents would make their kids idols in their lives. Their home life and even their own marriage would be superceded by meeting all the felt needs of the children. Family life revolved totally around their child instead of around Christ and the husband/wife relationship. And in the end, after high school graduation, the children—now adults—would reveal their real motives, and life became very difficult for the parents. Drugs, drinking and immorality became the way of life. And this was more than common for many people in my experiences.

In other passages we are told to love, cherish and teach our children, but never to put them first or above Christ. But here in this chapter, 1 Samuel 3, are examples of a parent's devotion to his children rather than his devotion to the Lord.

A BLIND EYE?

Eli was both a judge and priest in the worship center of Shiloh. This was about twenty miles north of Jerusalem in Ephraim. The Tabernacle and the Ark of the Covenant resided there (Joshua 18:1, Judges 18:31). The scene in 1 Samuel 1: 3 includes the presence of his two sons. This was quite unusual, and is as though the writer knew something of these two men, wanting to point out they were there also. As you read on in the story, these two sons of Eli turn out to be the scoundrels they have become known to be. It's also interesting to note that their actual names were Egyptian. Phinehas' name in Hebrew was Nubian, an Egyptian name derived from Nubia. Located in Egypt, modern day northern Sudan, this land had one of the harshest climates in the world. But Nubia was also a land of great wealth, of gold mines, ebony, ivory, exotic woods, precious oils, frankincense, and myrrh. Nubia was also a corridor to central Africa and a point for the trans-shipment of exotic goods from that region to the East. It may well have been due to these things and their influence that Eli gave his sons these symbolic names. But this also shows that even a priest/judge could be strongly influenced by these worldly cultures. You would think that a man of his religious position would have named them after Hebrew influences instead.

The name of his second son, the older of the two, Hophni, was also an Egyptian name, meaning "tadpole."

Throughout this passage, contrasts are developed between Samuel (who was also being raised by Eli), Hophni, and Phinehas.

- Samuel is seen as sincere, wholly devoted, pure, serving the Lord (2:11), whereas Hophni and Phinehas are shown as sinful priests, taking advantage of people (2:13-17);

How Not to Respond to Prodigals

- Samuel matures spiritually (2:18-21), while Hophni and Phinehas become more decadent (2:22-25);
- Samuel increases in stature and favor (2:26), while Hophni and Phinehas are marked for death because of their sinful hearts (2:27-36).

As Eli's religious influence declines over the course of time, Samuel's ministry emerges and develops. The astounding message of these passages involves young Samuel growing up in a house full of wickedness. Samuel, despite his family influences, *"was growing in stature and in favor both with the LORD and with men."* The writer immediately tells us what he thinks of Eli's two naturally born sons; they were *"worthless men"* (literally *"sons of worthlessness"*). He also states that they *"did not know the LORD"* meaning they did not regard God as their Lord and had no personal relationship with Him. Here were two grown men whose role it was to represent God and His holiness to the people, but in reality, under the external cloak of religion, were simply feeding their own lusts and using the temple to fulfill their evil desires. Eli's sons did not acknowledge God's moral authority over them; instead they did what was to their own advantage. So, here are three boys growing up in the same household with three different responses to God.

The texts also mention that, *"Eli was very old."* The age of Eli revealed his weakness and is compared to the youthful strength of Samuel (v. 26). Eli had resigned his own duties of his office to his two sons. Then the text reads that *"Eli heard."* Eli seems to be the last to hear, a fact that underlines his lack of engagement with his sons and that shows him as a poor leader for Israel and a poor example as a father. Eli was not even able to control his own appetites or his duties of watching over the sacredness of his office and of the behavior of his evil,

How Not to Respond to Prodigals

irreligious sons. These young men were taking sexual advantage of the women. The text reads they were fornicating with the *"women who served."* There is no reference to women serving at the temple in the Old Testament other than here. Service at the temple was reserved for Levite men. The implication is that Eli and his sons had somehow converted the temple into a pagan fertility shrine where the women would be prostitutes (see Deuteronomy 23:17).

Eli, guilty of putting his sons above God, should have known better to this sinful activity being allowed. We do know that such activity was common among the Canaanite religions, (see 1 Samuel 2:23-24), but not among the faithful Israelites. It is also evident that the Israelites viewed the behavior of Eli's sons as wicked. Eli, to some degree, did offer his admonition, though it was weak. Although he tells them they should not be doing this, he does not remove them from office as he should have. This lack of discipline and irreverence for the holiness and purity of God undermines any hope for restoration. Then the text reads that a *"man of God"* came to him. This is a designation for a prophet of God (see 1 Samuel 2:27-28). We are not told who this man is. Then the text reads to the *"Father's house,"* meaning the house of Aaron. Not all Levites could be priests but only those from the lineage of Aaron. The man of God then condemns Eli as well as his two sons.

These passages provide a stark contrast between the wickedness of Eli's sons and the righteousness of Samuel. Where did these sons go wrong, and how may they serve as a warning for all parents who read these texts?

- These sons were guilty of terrible greed and abuse of privilege. They had received great blessing and honor; yet they saw their sacred ministry as a means to take advantage of the very people they served. Many ministers,

How Not to Respond to Prodigals

in our day, labor under difficult circumstances and receive inadequate provisions for the proper support of the families; however, some ministers use their status as a means to unholy ends.

- In addition, these unworthy priests had a sinful disregard for their heritage as servants of the Lord. The text says that Hophni and Phinehas disregarded the custom of the priesthood concerning the collection of meat from the sacrificial altar. The Mosaic Law regulated some of this distribution, but the priesthood had established some helpful parameters for their work, and these sinful men had little respect for the servants who had gone before them. The Lord took notice of this disrespectful behavior and judged their actions.
- The sons also engaged in unspeakable acts, all in the name of God. Temple prostitution characterized much of the pagan religious practice of Canaan and Egypt, and these sinful sons incorporated these practices into the worship of Jehovah. They committed many sins of adultery and wicked compromise with false religious ways.
- Finally, Eli's sons refused to listen to the rebuke of their father. Perhaps years of leniency and compromise had dulled the boys' hearts to their father's requests; that's usually the case. Eli evidently compromised so much that he lost the moral discernment to correct his sons, and they refused to listen to his counsel.

All three boys received the same training from Eli, all three boys were raised in God's ways, and all three boys were surrounded from childhood by the religious influences of the Tabernacle. So how could two of them turn out to be so wicked while the third, Samuel, loved and served the Lord? Or, to bring the question closer to home, how come some of our sons and daughters serve the Lord while others do not? How come some of our sons and daughters love the Lord while others have hearts of stone?

Usually it is said that Hophni and Phinehas were so wicked and godless because their father was too soft. The truth is that Eli himself compromised the ministry by apparently allowing all the evil practices that were going on in it. If he had suddenly changed course and relieved his sons of the ministry he had previously allowed, he would have been seen by them as a hypocrite. He, too, would need to have resigned his office because of sin and a lack of integrity. This judgment upon all of them was due partly to Eli's lack of loving discipline (1 Samuel 3:13), his own compromise in obedience to God, his going along with the evil practices that were occurring, and his willingness even to receive the benefits of such sinful practices. Ultimately, however, he placed his love of his children above his love of God.

We also learned how he failed to discipline his boys when they were young, and refused to restrain them when they were older. We see that, in his lack of discipline, Eli failed his sons. Yet, as any parent can tell you, discipline by itself is not the answer—though it certainly is part of the answer. A couple of chapters later, the Bible tells us about Samuel as a father. Undoubtedly, he learned from Eli's mistakes and was a much better disciplinarian. Yet his sons did not walk in God's ways either (1 Samuel 8:3, 5). Even though the sons had a shining light of holiness living before them, they decided to walk in injustice and bribery, and were wicked judges before Israel. These times of bad judges, from Eli's sons to Samuel's, led Israel as a whole to set aside the rule of judges and created within them the desire to be like the other nations and have a king (see 1 Samuel 8:20). Why, then, is it that some children follow God's ways and others do not? Why the difference? They simply do *"not know the LORD."*

This is of key importance to the answer. The two sons of Eli had religious training, knew the laws and observances, yet decided in their own hearts to choose sin, all wrapped within a religious system. A text from Proverbs addresses this matter and tells us the reason for this all important difference: *"...by the fear of the LORD one keeps away from evil."* (Proverbs 16:6).

The difference lies in the persons themselves. Do they or do they not have any *"fear of the LORD"*? Those who fear the Lord do not lead a life of habitual evil. On the other hand, for those who do not fear the Lord, theirs is a heart of stone and a life of evil practices. When we consider Hophni and Phinehas, we see men who did not fear the Lord. The Bible tells us *"they did not know the LORD"*[4] (2:12). When this word is applied to God, it means to have a personal knowledge of Him, involving sincere worship, joyful obedience, true prayer, thoughtful Bible reading and practice, and the like. Hophni and Phinehas knew theologically about God, but did not know the Lord personally, and they did not fear the Lord. So, theirs was a life of evil and wickedness while even they served in the ministry. Samuel, on the other hand, did fear the Lord, did know the Lord, and so he faithfully served the Lord in righteousness. We have to be careful in distinguishing between knowing about a person and actually knowing that person.

Thanks to TV, newspapers, and magazines, we can know all about the President. Yet few of us know him personally. And the same can be true about God. In a typical Christian family, it is possible to know all about God. After all, we may have regular family devotions, attendance at worship services, church school, youth societies, Christian Schools, and personal devo-

---

[4] That is, they had no regard for the Lord.

tions. With all this, it shows that it is possible to know all about God without knowing Him intimately. Even Satan and all his thousands of demons know the Lord! Yes, they even have a greater reality of this knowledge than we have. Yet they are lost and all doomed to the lake of fire.

So, how are parents to react to such events? They need to realize some very important points—short and brief—about life and adult children who have become prodigals.

God's Sovereign Choice

This goes for our children as well. Since we don't know the mind of the Lord with respect to His work of election, our influence should always be used to urge them towards Christ. But we must realize that parents cannot save their children since saving faith is something that they themselves have to exercise. Eventually, all adult children must come to taking ownership of their own faith in Christ. We, as parents, cannot take on the role of the Spirit of God in saving people. We are to do our best, pray for the rest, leaving their lives in the hands of the Lord.

He chose us in Him before the foundation of the world. (Ephesians 1.4)

UNDERSTAND THIS: Ensure that you and your spouse focus on a close, sincere relationship to each other, where love, honesty, transparency, and biblical devotion to each other is strong.

Let the overflow of your relationship with each other and to Christ cascade as an influence towards your children. Be sure that you both have a personal, daily relationship with Christ.

God Can Be Trusted

Rest on the fact that God is sovereign, loving and altogether good. This is where the rubber hits the road in practice for any believer. I realize that we sometimes doubt this truth—that God is in complete control and is powerful enough to do what needs to be done. It's as though we feel we have to take over and play the part of the Holy Spirit. This is where faith plays a huge role for the believer—faith that God is real, and that He is working all things for the good of His children.

> *...also we have obtained an inheritance, having been predestined according to His purpose who works all things after the counsel of His will.*
> *(Ephesians 1:11)*

> *Truly I have spoken; truly I will bring it to pass.*
> *I have planned it, surely I will do it. (Isaiah 46:11)*

Honoring and Following God

This should not be done in any kind of hypocritical fashion, as with Eli. I would suggest sitting down with your spouse and, as honestly and openly as you both can, talk about anything that is not right between yourselves or in your lifestyles, based upon sound, biblical principles. Seek to follow the Lord out of a heart of pure love for each other and Him, living out the fruit of the Spirit in each other's lives. (See Galatians 5.)

Idols, He-dolls and She-dolls

I know this may be hard not to do. We spend years raising, loving and teaching them, many times pouring our lives into theirs. Then, as adults, they leave and appear to be worse sinners than those who are alien to all these things. A spiritually healthy perspective on all this is to see our children as a gift from God, yet a gift that brings the responsibility of having to be raised in a home where the overflow of the parents' own walk with the Lord is seen and taught.

Parents should never make their children the center of everything that goes on in the home but instead integrate them into the existing flow of home life as the family follows Christ. Otherwise idol worship occurs. This is where all is sacrificed for the children instead of attention being paid to other things in the home, especially the marriage relationship.

This was most vividly illustrated to me at a home school my children were part of for many years. Most of the kids I knew throughout the years were raised in a Christian home. But I noticed that there were several families that had made their kids the center of all home life. They poured a lot of time and money into their children over the years, many times sacrificing their own marriages and personal devotion to Christ. Soon after high school graduation, the real hearts of these same kids became a nightmare to these parents. Drunkenness, drugs and pregnancies outside of marriage followed. These kinds of situations can tend to harden the hearts of parents towards church, the Bible, and Christianity as a whole. This kind of response is not because of the truth about God or the Bible, but rather because their own little idols have turned on them in rebellion, and the parents find that they themselves have only a little foundation in their own relationship with Christ. The reality is that sinful motives of pride, control or some other heart attitude guided the parents throughout these years. And it created adult children living under the umbrella of their parents' religion, rather than the parents helping their children cultivate an independent, personal relationship with Christ and a corporate accountability to the local church for their lives. Part of parenting is raising our children to live independently of their parents in all areas of their lives—and this includes a faith they can ultimately own themselves.

5

How to Treat a Prodigal

How to Treat a Prodigal

Remember the parents' nightmare child, Bob? What are we to do in responding to people like Bob? That's an important practical question! Over the years I've seen two kinds of dangerous responses from people when it comes to the prodigal.

The first is to go to one extreme and treat the prodigal like a leper, cutting him off as though he had never existed. Most people do this because of hurt, anger, hiding from the church the situation for reputation's sake, or because they are fearful of what might happen due to their ignorance of what to do. Dismay fills their lives.

The second response some people have involves going to the other extreme and overlooking the prodigal's lifestyle choices and acting as though nothing has happened: there are no discussions about the critical issues in his life, no dealing with sin; just a glossing over, letting him do things to them that can eventually hurt financially, emotionally or even physically.

Let me give you some simple and workable guidelines that are effective; I know, because I've been through this myself with prodigals.

Firstly, Pray!

Pray that true salvation will come into his life and really bring about a change. Also pray for yourself, that God will teach and sanctify you through these ordeals. There is a spiritual battle going on over the souls of prodigals, and prayer is our tool in entreating God to do His divine will. There were times when Bob would actually say to others that he believed in God and that he was a Christian. But the fruit of his life showed otherwise. Jesus said of these kinds of people:

A good tree cannot produce bad fruit, nor can a bad tree pro-

duce good fruit. Every tree that does not bear good fruit is cut down and thrown into the fire. So then, you will know them by their fruits. (Matthew 7:18-20)

What our Savior is saying here is of vital importance when discerning if a person is a true believer. Anyone could hear what Bob said and actually think he was saved. Was he? Of course not! Even the demons believe in God (See James 2:19). A truly saved person will love the Lord, love to obey His principles, and have a love for others. Just believing in the existence of God only gives one a faithless assurance of salvation.

A Call to Turn

Prodigals may think they are Christians, but the reality is they are lost and stand under the wrath of God, just as with most of the world. You have to treat a prodigal as an unbeliever. How do you treat an unbeliever? By engaging in evangelism, and showing love and care. And this call to repentance is one to salvation, not just to reformation or a change in behavior. Salvation is not achieved by the work a person may do, but by the work of regeneration by the Spirit of God. What the prodigal needs is a reality check in his life as to his true standing before God.

This patient and discerning call to repentance should come from every Christian contact that the prodigal has—notably all those who are Christians in the arena of family or friends. I would strongly suggest that this unified approach should be discussed among all those affected. This is important. Here you have a person who may wrongly think he is saved, when in reality he is lost and will spend eternity in hell unless he truly turns. I've run across this kind of situation quite often. The prodigal's view of what a Christian looks like is twisted and warped.

How do you do this? This may be done lovingly by either talking to the prodigal alone or in a group setting. Some other things that could be done is leaving Bible-based materials to read or supplying a Bible. One of the most common actions family and friends take is to give their prodigal money or some kind of help that actually gives support to a lifestyle of drugs, alcohol or sex addiction. Sadly, prodigals in this situation sometimes have to hit bottom before they are willing to look up to God for help. Most of us simply will not change until affliction hits us personally. Only then will we be willing to seek a loving and patient Father.

> *"Because I called and you refused,*
> *I stretched out my hand and no one paid attention;*
> *And you neglected all my counsel*
> *And did not want my reproof;*
> *I will also laugh at your calamity;*
> *I will mock when your dread comes,*
> *"Then they will call on me, but I will not answer;*
> *They will seek me diligently but they will not find me,*
> *Because they hated knowledge*
> *And did not choose the fear of the LORD.*
> *"So they shall eat of the fruit of their own way*
> *And be satiated with their own devices.*
> *"But he who listens to me shall live securely*
> *And will be at ease from the dread of evil."*
> (Proverbs 1:24-33)

Your prayers and hopes are that they will realize that they are lost and will come to repentance, but in so many cases sin has become such a habit that it just seems natural to live as they do. When their physical needs are met, and when there is plenty of money in the bank, seeking God doesn't seem that important a thing to do. So, lies, deceit, theft, gossip, immorality and drunkenness are quite normal and, in a prodigal's thinking, seemingly not such a serious thing to God. In fact, some even have the idea that because they have suffered so much, God will have pity on them. Because He is a God of love, they say, He will somehow overlook their rebellion and let them into heaven. I've seen all these attitudes from people I've been in contact with.

But the way [that is, the lifestyle] of the ungodly shall perish. (Psalm 1:6)[5]

Practically speaking, all the sinful things they do become their god. They usually have some kind of idols of the heart that are foremost in their lives. These include sex, drugs, alcohol, material possessions, or a twisted view of freedom from God. I've also seen a multitude of people no longer attend church because their view of God was defined and influenced by the hypocritical actions of people they may have seen in the church or home. They embrace this fallacy because they do not realize God is not like man. The God of heaven is not their true father. Just because they know about God and believe He exists doesn't bring them into a saving relationship with Him.

"For My thoughts are not your thoughts, Nor are your ways My ways," declares the LORD.
(Isaiah 55:8)

---

[5] See also Psalms 37:20; 73:27; Luke 13:35, 1 Corinthians 1:18.

Do You Have a Responsibility toward the Prodigal?

Yes, you do. In a sense, you have the responsibility to pray for him, sharing the gospel and calling him to repentance. You are commanded to love him and to help him wisely when he has a true physical need. You are to be compassionate, gracious, and to have a willing heart to be a part of his life in bringing him back to the Lord.

As a Christian, you also have to trust in the sovereignty of God. When the parents of Bob unwisely continued to help him, they were showing a lack of trust in God and His dealings with people through affliction and foolish decision-making. As adults, they have the responsibility of caring for themselves. If they truly come to repentance, then, as a brother or sister, you have a responsibility to come alongside and help, but with a system of support and accountability in place. I've seen that prodigals who come to true repentance will want this system of accountability, whereas those whose repentance is false will shun it. If they truly come to the Lord, they will desire to come under a system of accountability involving either pastoral staff, or a family member or friend.

If any kind of addiction has occurred, I'd recommend a support and accountability system involving church leadership rather than family or friends because of the personal emotions and feelings that may otherwise arise. The prodigal will need to surrender his freedom for that season of time to learn what the Lord desires for him through this system of godly counsel and accountability. It may even mean putting him in a rehabilitation de-tox ward for a period of time.

A Prodigal Who Truly Repents Will Do This

There were many times Bob would hit bottom and he would then say he would change—if people helped. But in no way would he agree to be accountable to anyone. He wanted the help but he also wanted his freedom to sin. But a serious prodigal who has been saved will do anything at this point to please God. Consider the prodigal son in Luke 15:21. Upon his turning and repenting could he say, *"Father, I have sinned against heaven and in your sight; I am no longer worthy to be called your son."* A prodigal who isn't serious will say whatever it takes to use and abuse people, and will not be willing to come under accountability. Eventually, his life will become even worse, and it is at this point he may turn away. If you do see him again, warn him, yet with compassion, with sincere love, and with careful discernment, revealing to him the ugliness of his sin. Yet, understand this: you cannot take on the role of the Spirit of God. In the final analysis, the prodigal must be personally reconciled to God.

The way of the treacherous is hard. (Proverbs 13:15)

Adversity pursues sinners. (Proverbs 13:21)

The wicked flee when no one is pursuing. (Proverbs 28:1)

Your Pastor May Counsel You
Sadly, this is the one thing often not done when it comes to prodigals. Many families won't do this, perhaps because they feel embarrassed, ashamed, or maybe a lack of trust or fear of loosing their love. But realize that God Himself has placed them over you to be your shepherds. They may give you some insight you haven't thought about; and the local body of believers can pray for you and the people like Bob in your life. This is vitally important. This is the members of the

Body of Christ ministering to one another. Don't leave them out! They may help you see things more objectively. They are not there to hurt you but to give biblical guidance in these situations.

And He gave some as apostles, and some as prophets, and some as evangelists, and some as pastors and teachers, for the equipping of the saints for the work of service, to the building up of the body of Christ. (Ephesians 4:11-12)

Be on guard for yourselves and for all the flock, among which the Holy Spirit has made you overseers, to shepherd the church of God which He purchased with His own blood. (Acts 20:28)

God has placed gifted pastors over His people to guide and protect them throughout this life. That's why it is so important to listen to their counsel, entrusting your adult children to Him in situations like this. It may be that God has decided to use affliction, not only as a result of sin, but perhaps as a tool in bringing them to true repentance. It could well be that at certain times when a parent, sibling or friend rescues a prodigal from trouble, they are short-circuiting God's use of affliction in his life. At this point, let God do His work! Trust Him, continuing in your prayers for the prodigal, always willing to be used as a tool of the Lord in ministering to people like this.

Strength in Numbers

Get together with those who are connected with the troubled person's life, and discuss the issues. But first, carefully think through the group's plan of long-term actions. Discuss the problems while you are all together. Go over all the issues and create a plan you can all agree on—or at least one that the majority of you can agree on—on how to respond to the prodigal in biblical and loving ways.

What I've seen over the years is a mixed potpourri of bad decisions, in different ways, at different times where friends, family and others try to come up with ultimate solutions to save the prodigal, only to be let down over and over again. What may occur is that the prodigal uses his family and friends, in very devious and deceitful ways—even using guilt and sympathy—to get things from them. I've lost count of how many times I've seen this. What I am saying might seem cruel, but it's the truth. People need to realize that if a person is engaging in habitual sin, he will act that way too, even with family and friends.

> *But their minds were hardened; for until this very day at the reading of the old covenant the same veil remains unlifted, because it is removed in Christ. ...but whenever a person turns to the Lord, the veil is taken away.*
> *(2 Corinthians 3:14,16; see also 4:4, Isaiah 44:18.)*
>
> *You are of your father the devil, and you want to do the desires of your father. (John 8:44)*
>
> *Be shrewd as serpents and innocent as doves.*
> *(Matthew 10:16)*

Avoid Being Manipulated

What I'm about to say may also appear harsh but it is at this very point where most people fail, and prolong the troubled person's true need for a solution to his problems. Because of a lack of unity, discernment and patience in the support group, most people—especially the parents of the prodigal—give in when he cries wolf for facilities, food, and finance, only eventually to leave again in anger or disgust, and without even saying goodbye.

One such family member I knew went through this for several years with an adult child. When the prodigal finally hit the bottom of life and was living out in the streets, the parents came running to help, bringing the prodigal once again into their home; only to eventually go through many hardships until the prodigal again left.

This example repeats itself over and over again with family and friends, and yet it should not be the course for true believers. All they are doing is aiding a fool in his foolish ways, and prolonging their own hurt more as they try to help. A unified approach, one that is biblically informed and directed, is the best method. Does this mean then that if a group does this, repentance is guaranteed to be secured? No! There are no guarantees, but what it does is two things. *First*, it will protect the group trying to help from being used and therefore going through further emotional hurt, pain and financial hardships. *Second*, it will either bring about true repentance in the troubled person's life or he will muddle around in his sin until he passes from this earth. In this case, the reality is there is nothing you can do to save this troubled person; you can't play the part of the Holy Spirit. All you can do is what is outlined in this book and pray for the best, realizing God is doing a work of discipline in the prodigal's life, and a work of sanctification in yours.

One time I approached a man on the streets who I knew was in this situation. I made him an offer of housing, food and a job so he could get out of the mess he was in. He thought for a second and then said, *"No thanks, Mister, I don't want responsibil-*

ities and I like living out on the streets. This is my life." Those words didn't surprise me. Actually, I expected them. I have a family member who is often in and out of prison. Why? He is married and has several kids. His wife works to support them and when pressures come his way, such as all the responsibilities that come along with a family, he gets fed up, commits a crime and off to prison he goes for a year or two. There, he has free food, a bed, no responsibilities, and he can hang out with his homeless friends. Now, you might ask why his wife puts up with this. Well, to make things even worse, she thinks it's macho that he's an ex-con, as though he is tougher, and that's really cool and taught her kids that way too. Today, as adults, these same kids are in and out of jail, in gangs, and using drugs.

Troubled people most often, in reality, simply don't change, repent and come to Christ, even though it does happen at times. The pattern is that most stay in their sin all their lives, growing worse by the year until death takes its toll. You can't blame yourself for their choices. A simple rule is this: you can't take personal responsibility for their foolish choices any more than you can control the prodigal's choices. It's sad to say, but many people live with a false sense of guilt by not realizing this simple principle.

> *Because they hated knowledge*
> *And did not choose the fear of the LORD.*
> *"They would not accept my counsel,*
> *They spurned all my reproof.*
> *"So they shall eat of the fruit of their own way*
> *And be satiated with their own devices.*
> *"For the waywardness of the naive will kill them,*
> *And the complacency of fools will destroy them.*

*"But he who listens to me shall live securely
And will be at ease from the dread of evil."
(Proverbs 1:29-33)*

6

Coming to Grips with the Truth about Your Prodigal

Who Faces the Consequences?

This is where a lot of people get caught up emotionally with troubled people. They continue to harbor, feed, give money, and go through much emotional pain because they feel guilt, as though, even in a small way, it is their fault if they don't help. Moreover, the troubled person will feed off this false guilt, manipulating it and using it as a tool to sustain his sinful lifestyle.

But the reality is, it's all a lie. The prodigal is a grown and experienced adult who has chosen a sinful lifestyle and all its accompanying afflictions and, somehow, even though this lifestyle is twisted, finds a weird kind of security in it. Take some time and think about what he usually tells you. *"No one cares. Everyone is being mean and uncaring..."* These assertions all have something in common. It's everyone else's fault but theirs; it's as though the world should rotate around their needs and wants, and that includes you!

And that's the big problem of each prodigal: sin and self-centeredness. Until he humbles himself before God and repents, matters will only worsen with time, and there is nothing you can do. The Bible labels all who have rejected Christ and His ways as *fools and sinners*. This term is used for those who walk in habitual sin (even those who claim to be religious). Their lifestyle is one of sin, and foolish decision-making. The biblical term *"sinners"* is used for the lost, for those who walk in habitual sins rather than habitual righteousness, compared with the lifestyle of true believers. Do Christians sin? Yes, but they do not live a life of ongoing and habitual sin. A study of the Letter of 1 John reveals this quite clearly. Foolish people make foolish decisions, so you can't expect them to be wise! That's why a prodigal is called a sinner and a fool.

WHAT DOES GOD SAY ABOUT THIS?

- Sinners like to blame others for their problems (Genesis 3:12).
- Sinners like to blame groups of people for their problems (Exodus 32:21-24).
- Sinners like to claim to be innocent, even when they are living in sin (Matthew 27:24).
- Sinners like to claim ignorance for their sin when, in their hearts, they know exactly what they are doing (Acts 17:30-31).
- Sinners like to say they are good people and have done good to others in the past, therefore they should be helped now. This is a kind of usury—a payback for their previous "good deeds" (Exodus 33:12-13).
- Sinners like to blame their problems on their family ancestry or on the sins of others (Matthew 3:9-10). The truth is that God holds each person accountable for his or her own choices and lives.

The person who sins will die. The son will not bear the punishment for the father's iniquity, nor will the father bear the punishment for the son's iniquity; the righteousness of the righteous will be upon himself, and the wickedness of the wicked will be upon himself. (Ezekiel 18:20)

UNDERSTAND THIS: Realize that if you are helping them, they will create situations in the home that will give them excuses to leave your house and return to either the streets or someone else's house if they are called to be accountable.

I've had personal experience at this truth. We took care of a family member who had been living on the streets. Within several months, disputes, arguments and eventually the thankless departure of this prodigal left us all baffled. When situations like this occur, it makes people feel as though they have done something wrong. In reality, the prodigal wants help but he wants it without having to be accountable. For the troubled person, the last thing he wants to feel is that his leaving was his fault.

Remember, people like this think they are always in the right and that everyone else is wrong. This is a true victim mentality (see Proverbs 19:26; 20:20). When living an irresponsible lifestyle, one of the many responses from a prodigal is to create arguments, dissensions, and outbursts of anger or greediness within the home they are lodging. That gives them, they feel, an excuse to pack up and leave without notice, not even with a word of thanks for all the help they have received. And, as time passes, you may even hear that they are gossiping about you, saying how mean you had been towards them, and saying cruel words that you were selfish. Upon hearing this, you are stunned, wondering whom they were talking about. *"This isn't what happened,"* you may think! But still, they are gone.

The sad thing is that people who have hosted a prodigal often, without learning any lessons, let the same prodigal back into their home, and so they repeat the cycle many times. This causes further financial hardships, emotional strain, and more relational troubles. This is where wise discernment must be practiced, no matter how you feel. To help those who are not truly repentant of their sins is to ask for severe trouble in your home. What prodigals are actually saying is something like this: *"Let me in, accept my sinful lifestyle, and do not dare confront me with it."* They won't tell you this in so many words, but that's their expectation and that's how this cycle of dissention may be repeated in your home.

Drive out the scoffer, and contention will go out,
Even strife and dishonor will cease.
(Proverbs 22:10)

Let God Have His Way

This is where discernment needs to be exercised, not for your sake, but ultimately for the benefit of the troubled person. You must realize God is at work in that person's life, whether he is lost or saved. If the person is lost, God may be using afflictions as a tool to perhaps bring about true repentance. But if you repeatedly step in, you are relieving the pressure exerted by God in that situation. That is counterproductive. If the person is a Christian, but walking in habitual sins for a season, God is bringing discipline into his life in order to bring about repentance. So don't meddle in God's work! Let it take its course.

I know this is an area where wise discernment is sometimes hard to practice. You dearly care for the person, and you want to be used by God as an instrument to help, but at the same time you don't want to interfere with the workings of God. There is the question of balance. How do you reach out with love and grace, and at the same time let God do His work of discipline? This is where the church leadership can come alongside and help you, counsel you, and be supportive. We are to respond as God would have us. This may involve common grace, and we should pray for God's forgiveness to be shed on the prodigal. Keep in mind that if you do step in, you may be prolonging the suffering and making things worse. This is where true faith in God's power, sovereignty and discipline must be exercised. For many parents or friends, their tendency is to try and water down the sinful issues in the prodigal's life so as to somehow justify his evil acts. This allows the prodigal to reach out and receive help with seemingly little guilt. But minimizing the reality of sin is a dangerous thing to do.

> *He who says to the wicked, "You are righteous,"*
> *Peoples will curse him, nations will abhor him;*
> *But to those who rebuke the wicked will be delight,*
> *And a good blessing will come upon them.*
> *(Proverbs 24:24-25)*

Keeping Open Lines of Communication

Because he has chosen to walk in disobedience, it doesn't mean you are to stop loving and talking to him. When you do, make sure you objectively speak the truth, especially about the wrong decisions taken or about the sinful lifestyle, all in love and compassion. Listen well; speak carefully. *"He who gives an answer before he hears, It is folly and shame to him." (Proverbs 18:13)*. If the prodigal shares with you something he is doing that is wrong, lovingly explain, from the Scriptures, *why* it's wrong and what he should be doing instead. Many times prodigals are involved in sins such as immorality, lying, cheating, alcohol abuse, drugs or other illegal things, and they need to be told the truth. Be ready in season and out of season to graciously give an answer from the Bible on all these issues. If the prodigal does eventually repent and turn to Christ, he will thank you for your grace and objectivity with respect to his life when so many other people around watered down the true consequences of a sinful lifestyle.

> *My son, if sinners entice you, do not consent... My son, do not walk in the way with them. Keep your feet from their path. (Proverbs 1:10, 15)*

There is a way which seems right to a man, But its end is the way of death. (Proverbs 14:12 and 16:25)

A fool does not delight in understanding, But only in revealing his own mind. (Proverbs 18:2)

Don't give a prodigal money to pay late bills or to be bailed out of jail. All you are doing is allowing him to continue in his sins of irresponsibility. As a prodigal struggles through life, he should learn how to manage money, no longer wasting it and, as he becomes more responsible, no longer depending on others.

A man of great anger will bear the penalty, For if you rescue him, you will only have to do it again. (Proverbs 19:19)

This is the dilemma so many people have in trying to save their prodigals. They have to do it over and over again. Yet, prodigals show little repentance or desire to change. It is as if they expect others to conform to their own lifestyle of sin. During these seasons, a prodigal's love for sin is greater than his love for family, friends and he is especially likely to blame God. But deep in his heart, the sense of guilt is increasing. To suppress this, a prodigal will usually indulge in more sinful practices to try and cover it, getting lost in his own illusionary world of confusion.

Avoiding Blame-shifting
Gossip is a common sin with prodigals, so when he starts telling you about others, stop him and say it's wrong and that you will not participate. It's interesting to note that in the Bible, God says He hates several things and that one of them is gossip

(see Proverbs 6:19). Why? Because God's very nature is truth and truth telling. In the New Testament, the root of the word for gossip is the same as the one used for one of Satan's names—the accuser. Anyone who gossips is acting like Satan, the father of gossips, lies and deceit (Proverbs 6:17-19). If you are with the prodigal, show him through your speech and behavior your Christlikeness. This can be a witness of God's transforming power in a person's life. But if you falter and go along with the prodigal's conversation as though everything is OK, you have compromised your witness and are basically telling the prodigal, *"It's normal to walk in your sin and bring shame to so many people."*

One of the fallacies you could fall prey to is to think that you are the one special family member or friend who truly understands the prodigal and his problems. That's no more than an appeal to your own pride and self-centered glory. (See Proverbs 26:4-11.) You should not play the part of the Savior or the Holy Spirit; rather you are to point the prodigal to the Savior— the Lord Jesus Christ—to get out of his terrible plight. At these points, a Christian needs to use wise discernment in what the prodigal says or does, and respond biblically. You certainly don't want to think you're that one special person who understands the prodigal and his sin like no one else. What you are really being asked to do is to compromise your biblical values and let other people's sinful lives slide by unnoticed. You may be told things like *"You really understand me,"* or *"You're so caring,"* when in reality it is a ploy to suck you into their foolish situations. In no way is a believer to give in to such pride-infested schemes. Stand your ground lovingly, compassionately, and with biblical firmness. If you do take your stand, prepare yourself for the prodigal's rejection and probably outbursts of anger or a sad face of depression, *"A wicked man dis-*

plays a bold face[6]*"* (Proverbs 21:29a). If there comes a time in the future where the prodigal wants to repent and turn to God, he or she will return to those who spoke the truth in the first place.

Like apples of gold in settings of silver
Is a word spoken in right circumstances.
Like an earring of gold and an ornament of fine gold
Is a wise reprover to a listening ear.
(Proverbs 25:11-12)

He who guards his mouth and his tongue,
Guards his soul from troubles. (Proverbs 21:23)

Like a city that is broken into and without walls
Is a man who has no control over his spirit.
(Proverbs 25:28)

Hold, but Not Too Tight

What I mean by this is some prodigals are not going to change because, in a weird way, they like living the way they do. If you look at their relationships you will see them associating with other prodigals. They are those who have chosen to lead the same kind of lifestyle as your prodigal. You see them ever changing, acting irresponsibly, using deceit, greed and anger to solve their problems. Immorality and many other sins are theirs.

I remember so vividly one young man in our church whose father I was close friends with. The boy was raised in this church where strong biblical teaching and sweet fellowship

---

[6] (The analogy is that of a person hardening his face.)

Coming to Grips with the Truth about Your Prodigal

existed. But when the boy became an adult, he moved out and declared himself a homosexual. This grieved his father for several years. Much prayer went out for this young man. Eventually things turned for the worse, and life became very difficult for this prodigal. His family continued to show their love and care for him but stood firm as to his sinful lifestyle and often told him so. After several years had passed, the Lord brought such deep conviction and discipline to this prodigal that he repented and returned to the Lord. Today, he is a great witness to the homosexual community and involved in the church with his wife. In thinking about this young man's past, I am reminded of what James said. He talks about this kind of person and, from this, we see the picture of a modern-day prodigal.

[He is] . . . a double-minded man, unstable in all his ways. (James 1:8)

The Greek words used in the Letter of James speak about a person having his or her mind or soul divided between God's ways and the world's ways. This kind of person is a hypocrite who, on occasion, says he believes in God, yet shows no real faith, obedience, or genuine love for God. The Greek word for *"unstable"* comes from a verb which means, *"one who is never able to settle down."* Just like our prodigals!

So what is the path the prodigal should take? James again tells us. It's found here:

Submit therefore to God. Resist the devil and he will flee from you. Draw near to God and He will draw near to you. Cleanse your hands, you sinners; and purify your hearts, you double-minded. Be miserable and mourn and weep. . .

> *Humble yourselves in the presence of the Lord, and He will exalt you.*
> *(James 4:7-8)*

As a believer in relationship to the prodigal, you need to point him in the ways of Christ and His offer of salvation, guiding him away from his desperately lost plight.

This drawing near to God is an intimate pursuit of an intimate relationship with Christ on a daily basis (see Philippians 3:10). At this point in your prodigal's life, he has a casual relationship with God—an intellectual knowledge, much like demons have. They, too, believe in God, they know He exists, and know that His word is true. Everyone in hell has a relationship with God. Prodigals just don't want to see that they are sinners in the hands of a righteous judge who will judge them if they remain in their sins.

James says *"Cleanse your hands."* The reference to hands suggests one's lifestyle. The prodigal's lifestyle is dirty, sinful, unrighteous, and demanding God's wrath. In the Letter of James, God is commanding such people to come to Christ in faith, and have it as a goal to pursue holiness and purity in all aspects of life. But this can't be done in the flesh. You can't hold an unrighteous person responsible to obey God, or to walk in holiness. Holding such a person to this standard is fruitless. Why? There must first be a work of regeneration and the indwelling of the Holy Spirit must occur. But you can continue to share with the prodigal, lovingly and patiently, where he stands with God and the results of his life will be if he continues in this same direction. Perhaps longsuffering patience will be your ministry to this prodigal and God will give you strength and wisdom to endure. A sign of a true believer is his desire to please God in purity and righteousness. A merely religious person lives life on the edges, seeing how close it is possible to get to sin without being burned by it.

Then James says, *"Cleanse your hearts."* While the term *"hands"* speaks of external behavior; the heart symbolizes the motives, thoughts and desires. At the center of the prodigal's being is the lack of desire to deal with life and all its issues, good or bad, in biblical ways; thus he gathers up for himself more hardships. Because we live in a moral universe, created by a moral God, it is inevitable that there will be moral repercussions to sin. The way to change a prodigal's heart is certainly not though mere reformation, a changing of the lifestyle so as to be religious but still lost. Jesus condemned the religious leaders of His day for living such a way. Only as one comes to Christ, repenting of sins, willing to become a slave of Christ and living for Him above one's own desires, is one born again, regenerated and with a changed heart. (Read the following verses in reference to all this: Psalm 24:3-4, Jeremiah 4:4, Ezekiel 18:31, 36:25-26, I Timothy 1:5, 2 Timothy 2:22, 1 Peter 1:22).

Then in verse ten James closes with this instruction: *"Humble yourselves in the presence of the Lord."* This is where the prodigal must go. He should not be proud, not with a list of demands, and not with complaints, but rather, realizing where he stands before a holy God and humbly coming to Him for mercy. As has been seen, this is what killed Aaron's two sons, and it will bring hell to every prodigal who refuses to come to God this way.

7

Whose Fault Is It?

Whose Fault Is It?

So whose fault is it?[7] Parents ask this question many times: "Where did I go wrong?" Parents who raised their kids in a Christian home—did they do their best? Were they perfect? Probably not! We do our best, and yet the kids grow up and completely walk away from the Lord and want nothing to do with Him. We shake our heads and within our soul find ourselves asking questions such as these: What did I do that was wrong? Is it my fault?

Apportioning Blame

But the better question to ask is this: "Who's responsible for their own soul?" There may have been things you, as a parent, did wrong—just like every other parent raising children has done—but we mostly do our best. And as an adult, each child is responsible for his or her own decisions. When it comes down to it, individual grown-up children must take ownership of their salvation and this is a critical stage for every human being alive. You can't point your finger to your parents, your church, or any other negative experience in your background. Rather, all adult child prodigals will one day stand before God, the Creator the universe, and have to give an account of the lives they lived and the decisions they took.

Salvation is ultimately a single ownership decision made by every single adult prodigal. So for many parents, the guilt that we may carry around with us for many years—blaming ourselves for the adult prodigal's decisions they made—is not ours to carry. These are personal responsibilities that do not belong to us. Every decision the adult child makes is his or hers alone.

---

[7] Data from Dr. John Street's Sunday school class, Grace Community Church, July, 2015

Whose Fault Is It?

Our adult prodigals will be held accountable for those decisions, whether morally, spiritually or legally.

Sometimes parents cling to Proverbs 22:6 as some kind of spiritual promise, where Solomon says, *"Train up a child in the way he should go; even when he is old he will not depart from it."* As parents we cling to this verse thinking along these lines: "If I raise my child in a Christian home, he'll turn out to be a Christian adult, right?"[8]

You need to realize that nothing is guaranteed in this life. We live in a fallen world that's been cursed, and there are so many negative influences both inside and outside the heart, that each person must come to a point in life where he or she makes the personal decision as to whether or not to follow the Lord, no matter what kind of childhood influence there may have been.

As we'll see shortly, a child could be raised in a home full of evil influences and yet come out following the Lord, or he could be raised in a godly home and choose not to follow the Lord. The bottom line for this is rebellion in the heart—a rebellion of the prodigal and that is centered on selfishness. If a child truly wants to live a life of habitual sin in this world, he will do so, no matter what home life lies in the background. To simply blame it on the parents in the home is too naïve and simplistic.

To add clarity to this Bible verse, Proverbs 22:6 is not a promise. It does not promise parents that if they raise their kids in a godly home, they will turn out as Christians. The actual Hebrew in this verse reads, "Dedicate a child upon the mouth of his way and when he is old he will not depart from it." This verse is a warning. It's important to realize that many

---

[8] The Master's College Counseling Course, *Proverbs and Counseling*, 2005

Whose Fault Is It?

verses in the Book of Proverbs are not given as a hard and fast promise, but as a general principle for how a way of life may work out.

So what does "mouth of his way" mean? The behaviorist psychologist, Dr. B. F. Skinner, believed that if you established the right environment, the creature will turn out according to the environment you created—good in, good out[9] or, as Albert Bandura taught, children learn positive and negative behavior from their parents and thus you can predict how they will turn out.[10] But that's not how the human heart works. Yes, you dedicate your children individually to the Lord but they're going to follow their own way eventually, and they're going to do their own thing. So when they grow up and do whatever they want, following their own sinful nature, the repercussions may well be a prodigal lifestyle or they may choose to walk with the Lord, taking ownership of their own relationship to Christ. That should be the parents' focus.

Sinful Nature

The influences of the sinful nature are extremely strong and ever-growing and such influences can only be changed when a heart is transformed by the Spirit of God. Every single child that grows up must come to the point of taking ownership of his or her own relationship in a daily walk with Christ, becoming convicted of the need to follow Him. You could be a perfect parent and yet that child could still turn away. An example of this is found in Isaiah 1:2. Here God, the perfect parent, says of His child Israel, *"Listen, O heavens, and hear, O earth; for the*

---

[9] Information from *Essentials of Understanding Psychology*, 8th edition, Robert J. Feldman, 1987, 396-397
[10] Ibid., 397

LORD speaks, 'Sons I have reared and brought up, but they have revolted against Me'." Here you have the perfect parent raising His own children—personified in the nation of Israel—and giving them everything they need. He provides not only nourishment but also truth, and yet they still reject Him. Is God, then, at fault? Never! God is perfect in all His ways and He does everything exactly right. God didn't fail; it was the heart of His children. Just like this verse, Proverbs 22 is a call for parents to jump into the child's life and to bring a strong warning. You graciously, lovingly and patiently teach children and warn them about the influences on the sinful things of this world but ultimately they must make their own decision as to which way they're going to follow. My personal advice is for parents to sit down with their kids daily and go through the book of Proverbs, explaining to them both the blessings of following the Lord and also the warnings of living a foolish lifestyle as a prodigal.

There are many proverbs to be found in the Bible. One of them is found in Ezekiel 18:2. One of the most common things prodigals do is shift the blame and complain, and Israel was no different—and they were still God's children. The people of Judah would not acknowledge their own guilt though they themselves were very wicked and idolatrous. Instead of taking ownership of their own decisions, they blamed their forefathers for the state of suffering they were living in. They tried to rationalize their poor state, one that was expressed in a very common proverb of that time. In Ezekiel 18:1-4, these words are recorded:

Then the word of the LORD came to me, saying, "What do you mean by using this proverb concerning the land of Israel, saying,

Whose Fault Is It?

> *'The fathers eat the sour grapes,*
> *But the children's teeth are set on edge'?*
> *As I live,"* declares the Lord GOD, *"you are surely not going to use this proverb in Israel anymore. Behold, all souls are Mine; the soul of the father as well as the soul of the son is Mine. The soul who sins will die."*

They thought because their fathers had sinned (eaten sour grapes), the result was that they were suffering because of them (and thus their teeth were on edge). In the Bible, God expresses several times things that He hates, and this is one of them:

There is a sense in which God hated this proverb because of the way His people accused Him of being at fault for their problems when in reality it was their own individual decisions that had brought about their problems. Children were not getting punished for their parent's sins by God. Yes, there could be the repercussions of a parent's lifestyle influences upon the children—whether in finances, relationships, and so forth but what it comes down to lies at the heart, the focal point is that of the issues and decisions that each adult child makes in responding and reacting to life.

There are thousands of examples of people who have come out of a not-so-good a home life and made something of themselves—greatly—hence the teaching of verses 5-9.

> *"But if a man is righteous and practices justice and righteousness, and does not eat at the mountain shrines or lift up his eyes to the idols of the house of Israel, or defile his neighbor's wife or approach a woman during her menstrual period—if a man does not oppress anyone, but restores to the debtor his pledge, does not commit robbery, but gives his*

> *bread to the hungry and covers the naked with clothing, if he does not lend money on interest or take increase, if he keeps his hand from iniquity and executes true justice between man and man, if he walks in My statutes and My ordinances so as to deal faithfully—he is righteous and will surely live," declares the Lord GOD."*

When you look at Ezekiel 18, you see examples of good homes with bad kids, and bad homes and good kids. In verse 10, there is mention of a son who is raised in a godly home and grows up, becoming a robber and murderer. And in verse 13 God says "he shall surely die, his blood shall be upon him." Even though this son was raised in a godly home, he chose to rebel and he suffered the consequences. God says that he shall be held personally responsible for his decisions. But then in verse 14, there is the opposite—a son who is raised in a home where the father habitually sinned and was not godly, and the son saw all of this and he considered all his ways and he decided to follow the Lord. He does not follow in the examples and influences of the sinful father but he decides to personally follow the Lord and stay away from those things. In a verse 17, God promises that he shall surely live.

Accountability

> *The person who sins will die. The son will not bear the punishment for the father's iniquity, nor will the father bear the punishment for the son's iniquity; the righteousness of the righteous will be upon himself, and the wickedness of the wicked will be upon himself. (Ezekiel 18:20)*

Whose Fault Is It?

It is clear from verse 20 that individual accountability is the rule of the universe. That's why God says repercussions in decisions that are made by adult prodigals in this life are their decisions rather than those of their parents or friends. But then in verse 24 there is an example of a person who once walked with the Lord and now turns away.

"But when a righteous man turns away from his righteousness, commits iniquity and does according to all the abominations that a wicked man does, will he live? All his righteous deeds which he has done will not be remembered for his treachery which he has committed and his sin which he has committed; for them he will die. Yet you say, 'The way of the Lord is not right.' Hear now, O house of Israel! Is My way not right? Is it not your ways that are not right? When a righteous man turns away from his righteousness, commits iniquity and dies because of it, for his iniquity which he has committed he will die. Again, when a wicked man turns away from his wickedness which he has committed and practices justice and righteousness, he will save his life. Because he considered and turned away from all his transgressions which he had committed, he shall surely live; he shall not die. But the house of Israel says, 'The way of the Lord is not right.' Are My ways not right, O house of Israel? Is it not your ways that are not right?

"Therefore I will judge you, O house of Israel, each according to his conduct," declares the Lord GOD. "Repent and turn away from all your transgressions, so that iniquity may not become a stumbling block to you. Cast away from you all your transgressions which you have committed and make yourselves a new heart and a new spirit! For why

will you die, O house of Israel? For I have no pleasure in the death of anyone who dies," declares the Lord GOD. *"Therefore, repent and live." (verses 24-32)*

1 Corinthians 10:13 states that *"no temptation has overtaken you accept such as common to man; but God is faithful, who will not allow you to be tempted beyond what you are able, but with the temptation will also make the way of escape, that you may be able to bear it."* As you can see from the short study of Ezekiel 18 all individuals are accountable for their own decisions. No one can ever point a finger at parents or friends before a Holy and just God and say it was their fault. But it must also be realized that the sins of the parents can have a very negative influence on children. However, ultimately, all adult children must take responsibility for their own life choices.

But in all this, God's nature is one of love and forgiveness, showing that He takes no pleasure in bringing judgment or death upon people. That's why, in verse 21, God says in all of these situations, *"But if the wicked man turns from all his sins which he has committed and observes all My statutes and practices justice and righteousness, he shall surely live; he shall not die."* Here God offers complete forgiveness for any sins committed.

As parents, we have to realize the true nature of any child—a nature that is bent toward sin. I raised four children and I've seen firsthand that they didn't need to learn in the home how to be selfish, lie or show anger. It was all in their little hearts from the beginning. And it takes the work of the Holy Spirit to bring about transformation in such a life. We are not ourselves to take the role of the Holy Spirit, and we have no direct part in that miracle of grace that He works. Children are a gift from the Lord, on loan to us, and once they reach adulthood, they take on more personal responsibilities and decisions. The focus of the home should never be the children but the marriage relationship because that is permanent—whereas the task of raising children ordinarily comes to an end when they reach adulthood. The goal is to raise them and let them go on their own to start their own families, not to hold on to them permanently.

Letting Go

Sometimes parents have a hard time letting go, and they tend to develop a skewed view about their children—that somehow they are generally good and righteous, and that whatever decisions they make as adults become justified as good, even when they are, in fact, bad decisions. It's important to realize the profound truth of what Proverbs 22:15 says. "Foolishness is bound up in the heart of a child but the rod of correction will drive it far from him" That *is* true. By nature every child is bent toward rebellion, to one degree or another. Many times the view that we take of our own adult children is quite different from God's. Why? Because God sees the heart and His judgments are right and fair, whereas the perspectives that parents may have are skewed because of their love for their children. This alone may influence us to have a wrong view of our child's decisions and actions. We all need to establish an accurate view of our adult children so that we may have something of the same understanding that God has.

When Children Become Adult Prodigals

In the first place, God says that children are all naturally foolish and they are all bent on rejecting Him. Proverbs 22:15 states that foolishness is bound up in the heart of a child. And when children grow up, this foolishness grows up with them, to the point that they may become arrogant and hardened in sin.

They're foolish and will naturally make foolish decisions. As the old saying goes, "An apple tree bears apples, a peach tree bears peaches, and foolish people make foolish decisions." So if any prodigal rejects God, He calls such a person foolish. Psalm 14:1 records that "the fool has said in his heart there is no God." The word in Hebrew "fool" is *naval*, and means morally insensitive. Prodigals are foolish people who are morally insensitive to God's ways and do not take into account the repercussions of their personal decisions.[11]

Second, children are naturally fickle, and they drift away from God's instructions. They have a natural and prominent waywardness in their hearts, and tend to drift away toward a sinful lifestyle. Proverbs 19:27 reads "Cease listening to instruction my son, and you will stray away from the words of knowledge." The role of the parent is to straighten out this waywardness by exercising and applying truth and discipline. However, once such children reach adulthood, they—and not their parents—become responsible for the way they should go. If you are a parent, your role now shifts from that being a guardian to that of a prayerful observer—and, as such, you have to exercise much prayer, counsel and patience.

Third, a child's focus from birth is naturally self-focused. Children are born seeing themselves as the center of the universe with all their needs being speedily and conveniently met by everyone around them. As they grow up, they must be taught that they are *not* the center of the universe, but ones who are growing to be no longer self-focused, and, rather, others-focused. Kids will naturally view their own ways in a self-

---

[11] The Master's College Biblical Counseling Class, *Proverbs and Counseling*, Will Simmons, 2014

favoring way, and tend to be self-reliant.[12] Sometimes they may believe there is a God (but only consider Him as needed in times of crisis), and maintain their perspective that they are the center of the universe. Proverbs 16:2 states that "all the ways of a man are pure in his own eyes, but the Lord weighs the spirits." Titus 1:15 says "To the pure all things are pure, but to those who are defiled and unbelieving nothing is pure; but even their own mind and conscience are defiled." Prodigals are corrupt on the inside (in their mind and consciousness) and on the outside (as seen in their works and disobedience). Proverbs 16:2 clearly shows us that while people can be self-deceived, God discerns their true motives and will judge them according to their personal decisions.

Fourth, a child's forgetfulness is very natural because of his or her depravity. Since every person born is sinful, sin will naturally flow out as a result of the ensuing attitudes in life decisions. Proverbs 4:5 reads "Get wisdom! Get understanding! Do not forget, nor turn away from the words of my mouth. Do not forsake wisdom, and wisdom will preserve you." The role of the parents is to continually teach their children the way of the Lord—not from threats or by forcing their views down their throats, but to graciously and lovingly show them by word and deed. Life example in the home speaks louder than words. Parents should make sure there is no contradiction between the two.

Fifth, a child's fear of God is naturally just not there. Children don't take into account the consequences of their decisions, they are shortsighted, and they rarely think long-term. If I were to go to one of my grandchildren and ask them, "Would

---

[12] Ibid.

you like $10 now or $10,000 one year from now?" which one do you think they would choose? Most would choose the $10 and not think long-term. Kids are that way. And as they grow up, many adults don't take into account the consequences of their decisions, and many times they face the repercussions of those bad decisions in legal, financial, moral, or relational terms. Yet, God is faithful and just, loving and gracious, and many times uses those decisions made by prodigals to come back upon them as a tool to bring about repentance. And as a parent, sometimes you may have to back off, let go, and let God do His work so as to bring repentance—even if that may only be tomorrow, next month, or years from now.

Sixth, children can naturally recognize hypocrisy in the home. Everyone is born with a God-given conscience and therefore knows something of right and wrong. Romans 2:14 – 16 refers to the God-given conscience. And when children grow up in a Christian home where there is hypocrisy—they see their parents saying one thing and living a lifestyle different from what they profess—what they conclude is that there is hypocrisy. And they also naturally conclude that Christianity is fake, so they tend to perceive God in like manner, considering Him like man. Your actions will speak louder than your words.

Seventh, it's important to realize that sometimes prodigals become adults and intentionally choose a lifestyle of habitual sin, ending up with a seared conscience. They have been so exposed to sin, and they practice sin so habitually that their guilt is silenced. What I mean by this is that a person's God-given conscience is a warning light that flashes when something morally wrong is done. But if a prodigal moves on and makes a decision to continue living in habitual sin, the result is a seared conscience. The Word of God is clear: 1 Timothy 4:2 states "Now the spirit expressly says that in later times some will depart from the faith, giving heed to deceiving spirits and doctrines of demons, speaking lies in hypocrisy, having their own conscience seared with a hot iron..." The Greek word for "seared" is a medical term referring to cauterization. The lives of prodigals are full of hypocrisy and lies because their consciences have been desensitized. It is as if all the nerves of the conscience that make them feel bad or good have been destroyed and reduced to scar tissue by the burning desires of habitual sin. The consciences of prodigals are referred to in Ephesians 4:18 where the apostle Paul spoke of *"having their understanding darkened, being alienated from the life of God, because of the ignorance that is in them, because of the blindness of their heart; who, being past feelings, have given themselves over to lewdness, to work all uncleanness with greediness."* Prodigals are morally insensitive, even to the cries of their parents. If they won't listen to God, they are not going to listen to their parents. And they will continue to sin in turning away from God, to the point that they become still more apathetic about moral and spiritual things. God has given us this consciousness—this awareness—as a warning beacon, and guilt thus becomes clearly identified. Prodigals eventually kill their guilt as seared and repressed. Parents in this situation need to be patient, loving towards them, and to trust in the Lord, no matter the outcome.

Eighth, it is important as a parent to realize that raising a child in a child-centered home often produces prodigals. Why? Because the child becomes an idol. I have seen this often in the case of children who are home schooled. Let me make it clear that I am not against home schools—my wife and I raised two of our four kids in home school, and my wife was a great teacher. But for some homes, the child becomes the centerpiece and actual idol of the home. Many times, such a child is used by one of the spouses as a way to avoid the other spouse. Biblically the only thing permanent thing in the home is the marriage relationship—the kids are just passing through on a what is ultimately a temporary basis. Our goal as parents is to raise them so as to be people who wish to follow the Lord and are able to make independent decisions on their own and eventually to live on their own, raising their own families. Genesis 2:24 reads "Therefore a man shall leave his father and mother and be joined to his wife, and they shall become one flesh." The marital relationship was established as the first human institution. Now the responsibility to honor one's parents does not cease with leaving and cleaving to one's wife or husband. But when a person does leave and cleave, this represents the inauguration of a new and primary responsibility. "Joined" carries a sense of a permanent relationship and "one flesh" speaks of a complete unity of parts making a whole, one cluster, one union. Thus the marital union is, in this regard, complete and whole with two people. Once the kids grow up and become adults who leave the home, the only thing left is the permanent marriage relationship. It's at this point where marriages may fall apart because the idol moves out. So this idol lives the lifestyle of an idol, one filled with self-fulfilling activities, self-centeredness, self-reliance, and a sense of not needing God. Then all is quiet, the idol is gone, and the parents are once again left alone to face each other and the reality of their broken marriage relationship. The parents' own relationship was not developed throughout the years of raising their children, so they have nothing to fall back on.

Ninth, sometimes children are raised in homes where they are exasperated; they may turn out as adults who reject Christ. I once counseled some parents who were very legalistic, and this strictness left their son with a lot of bitterness that spilled over into his adult life. Such is an example of a Christian home where the kids have been so mistreated and abused under the name of Christ that they in like manner interpret God through the lens of the hypocrisy of their parents, seeing Him in terms like them—cruel and mean—and thus wanting nothing to do with a god like that. They live perhaps with a lot of rules and regulations, a home not filled with love, understanding, patience, forgiveness, but instead with parents who seem more like dictators, unbinding, giving no encouragement, and who merely dispatch harsh discipline. There is no loving respect. So they naturally come to the view that God is harsh, mean, and ready to beat them over their heads. It is critical that in their home, parents live a life of grace, love, orderliness, patience, showing forth what a Christian marriage is to look like. It is interesting to note that in the New Testament, both Jesus and the Pharisees confronted people. The Pharisees were strict and harsh, and set the standard for people to meet, or else be punished. They were cruel, harsh and impatient, with no love. Jesus, on the other hand, showed common people love, forgiveness, and the way to receive the blessings of God. So the parents must do to their children.

Tenth, sometimes children may be raised in a church where they see duplicity from people in the congregation. They may see other parents who are hypocritical, gossips, mean-spirited and judgmental. Ultimately, interpreting God according to the actions of other people leads to a skewed and wrong understanding of God. My own father had this experience. Eventually, though, he realized that God was not like his parents, and he came to Christ at an older age.. Prodigals still have the choice to find out from the Bible who God really is. Yes, there may be negative influences all around them, but ultimately God will hold them accountable for the decisions they make. Your goal as a parent is to live a godly loving and gracious lifestyle before your kids, showing them the ways of Jesus in biblical terms.

Eleventh, sometimes parents can be too lenient. There's a good example of this in 1 Kings 1:5 where it is recorded that "then Adonijah ... exalted himself, saying 'I will be king'; and he prepared for himself chariots and horsemen, and 50 men to run before him." Then there's a note by the author in parentheses that says "and his father had not pained him at any time by saying, why have you done so?" Apparently David did not discipline him throughout his growing up years so he rebelled, and David suffered much. It's also interesting to note that his younger son, Solomon, was raised quite differently. He was disciplined and taught by David. Undoubtedly David learned his lesson through the experience of his older son, Adonijah, and wanted to follow a different approach with his son Solomon. In Proverbs 4:3, Solomon says of David, his father, "When I was my father's son tender and the only one in the site of my mother he also taught me and said to me 'Let your heart retain my words keep my commands and live.'" The word tender means vulnerable. Solomon, through David's influence, allowed himself to be open to the teachings of God; and during his younger years, he did follow that.

HOPE FOR PARENTS

Now that we've seen all that's in play when it comes to adult prodigals, along with all the disheartening things that could possibly happen to our children when they make their bad decisions, I don't want to leave the reader there. I want you to understand that with God there's always hope, hope that God will bring them back to the faith. This may not be today or tomorrow—but eventually! Ezekiel 18:21 gives us that hope. As parents we watch our prodigals do things and make decisions that we—as Christians—know are destructive to themselves sometimes financially, relationally, spiritually, emotionally and maybe legally. We watch as sin backfires on them because of their wrong decisions and, as parents, we hurt, pray and hope that the light will come on once more in all they've been taught. But with patience we must continue to pray and hope. In verses 21-23, God says

> *"But if the wicked man turns from all his sins which he has committed and observes all My statutes and practices justice and righteousness, he shall surely live; he shall not die. All his transgressions which he has committed will not be remembered against him; because of his righteousness which he has practiced, he will live. Do I have any pleasure in the death of the wicked,"* declares the Lord God, *"rather than that he should turn from his ways and live?"*

8

The Real Issue: Jesus as Master

The Real Issue: Jesus as Master

We've covered a lot of ground so far in the book but now we come to the very crux of the issue—the question that asks who is Master: Self or the Lord Jesus Christ? This is always the issue, for everyone born, as it involves one's eternal destiny.

Today, many people profess to be Christians. And, as you look around, there seem to be all kinds of Christians. Turn on the TV and the picture you have is a happy, self-willed, wealthy and healthy person whose life is directed seemingly by God meeting his or her every whim. Moreover, today, people actually define what it means to be a Christian. God, they say, is our pal, our buddy, a god whose goal it is to satisfy our desires. We are told that this is also a god who has become much more merciful than ever so in the Old Testament, and who no longer takes sin as a serious matter. This god, it is believed, dispenses blessings without obligation. So, if you name it, claim it, and visualize it, it will come about. Is this really the God of the Bible?

This may come as a surprise but, no, God is not like this, even though we see this kind of picture being presented from many pulpits and TV shows today. He is not our personal buddy, our pal, and definitely not our waiter, standing by to please our selfish desires. Instead, He is Lord, Master and God of all creation who has laid out in Scripture what a true believer is really like. That's what I'm about to challenge you with now. It won't be easy, and it definitely goes against what you may hear and see today. So let's look at the Bible and see what God's definition of a true Christian is. Let's start off by looking at John 13:12, 13.

"Do you know what I have done to you? You call Me Teacher and Lord; and you are right, for so I am."

The Real Issue: Jesus as Master

Here Jesus clearly calls Himself Lord. The Greek word is *"kurios"* and it carries the idea of one who has power, absolute authority, a total right to control. It's a very powerful term, used of Him being God, Master of all. This word is used 747 times in the New Testament. This concept—that Jesus is God, and that He rules as Lord—has largely been set aside in modern expressions of Christianity, to the extent that He is diminished to the level of a servant awaiting our slightest commands. But this is quite the opposite of God's view. Jude warns us about people who water down the lordship of Christ.

For certain persons have crept in unnoticed, those who were long marked out for this condemnation, ungodly persons who turn the grace of our God into licentiousness and deny our only Master and Lord, Jesus Christ. (Jude 4)

But false prophets also arose among the people . . . who will secretly introduce destructive heresies, even denying the Master who bought them.
(2 Peter 2:1)

Since Jesus is our Lord and Master, that naturally leads us to the conclusion that He has slaves. During the times that Jesus used this terminology, slavery was a normal part of life, and was fully accepted. Jesus neither condemned it, nor condoned it. And it was the same, too, with the apostles. Jesus used this living metaphor to paint a picture of what it would take in the minds of those who wanted to follow Him. A master is not a master unless he has slaves; that's obvious. If Jesus is Master, who would His slaves be? Those who desired to become a slave of Christ. Since the people of Jesus time were fully immersed in a culture of slavery and the words used to

The Real Issue: Jesus as Master

describe it, it's not surprising we see so much of it being used as a picture of true Christians.

We are slaves and He is the master. That's the imagery Jesus wanted to convey to His true followers. So what does a slave look like? He or she has no rights, and no options to be obedient or not. Whatever the master says, the slave does. That's why Jesus' words caused many who heard Him to walk away; they knew exactly what He was talking about. His constant sayings of *"Take up your cross and follow Me"* sent a clear message that He was to be obeyed (see Luke 9:23).

Let's now take a tour through the New Testament and see what it means to be a slave of Christ. But I must warn you, most Bible translations today don't use the word "slave" because of its negative connotations. Instead, they translate the word *"doulos"* as "servant" or "bondslave." We are not servants. Servants have options, they get paid, they can choose whether or not to work for their master, and they can leave to go back home after their work is finished. Instead, by biblical contrast, we actually are slaves![13]

> *If you confess with your mouth Jesus as Lord, and believe in your heart that God raised Him from the dead, you will be saved. (Romans 10:9)*

These are powerful words. You have to confess from your heart that Jesus is your Master and Lord, which therefore means you are willing to become His slave, willing to be obedient to His desires, and even willing to die for Him. We are asked to give up our own personal dreams and ambitions, and

---

[13] For an excellent treatment of this topic, see John MacArthur, *Slaves—The Hidden Truth About Your Identity In Christ*, Nashville, Thomas Nelson, 2010.

The Real Issue: Jesus as Master

submit ourselves to a will that is not our own. For twenty-first-century westerners this is a hard concept to accept. But in Jesus' times, it was fully understood by those around Him. The Old Testament saints knew this (Acts 2:18), the apostles knew it (Acts 4:28-29), and the demons even knew they were slaves (Acts 16:17). Pastors and elders of the church knew they were slaves (Colossians 4:7, 2 Timothy 2:24). Even the Apostle John, writing about the future, knew there would be slaves of Christ (Revelation 1:1; 7:3; 10:7; 19:2). At the end of time, when all the future judgments have occurred, we will be slaves of God, serving Him forever (Revelation 22:3, 6). Paul the Apostle saw himself as a slave (Romans 1:1), as did James (James 1:1), Peter (2 Peter 1:1), Jude (Jude 1) and John the Apostle (Revelation 1:1).

But this picture is even richer for the true believer. Our Master is not like some cold, unloving Greek deity who is a harsh taskmaster; instead, He is one so full of grace and love for us, to the extent that He Himself was willing to die in our place of judgment. The Scriptures make it clear that we were called and chosen (see Ephesians 4:1). They picture a master going into the marketplace and buying a slave or two from among the many. This is the picture of believers chosen by Christ before the foundation of the world. However, the Master had to pay a price. What price was God willing to pay for His elect, the chosen slaves that would serve Him? His own life. In fact, Jesus was willing to become a slave Himself on your behalf. Consider what Paul says about this:

Have this attitude in yourselves which was also in Christ Jesus, who, although He existed in the form of God, did not regard equality with God a thing to be grasped, but emptied Himself, taking the form of a bond-servant, and being made in the likeness of men. Being found in appearance as a man, He humbled Himself by becoming obedient to the point of death, even death on a cross. (Philippians 2:5-8)

So our Master became a slave of obedience to the Father, even to the very point of death. This is what defines a true Christian—obedience to the Master. The Master commands; his slaves obey (read John 15:10, 12, 14, 17). But Jesus goes one step further, and He calls us *friends*. We are slaves but we are intimately close to our Master because He has revealed His will to us. In biblical terms, anyone who is a true Christian lovingly and willingly obeys Christ and what He commands, and does so from a willing heart of love for the One who saved him from the market place of sin and destruction.

If you keep My commandments, you will abide in My love; just as I have kept My Father's commandments and abide in His love. (John 15:10)

You are My friends if you do what I command you. (John 15:14)

But we have the mind of Christ. (1 Corinthians 2:16)

To us His slaves, God has revealed to us what He desires (John 15:14-16). In Jesus' day, this concept of a slave being a friend of the master was very rare. It was reserved only for slaves that were very close to the master and who knew what he wanted. They were called his friends because he revealed his will to them. Today, we have the wholly known counsel of God, the Bible, revealing the mind of the master to His slaves—to us who are His friends. His slaves are known for their obedience. And as far as His slaves are concerned, the Master fully expects them to be obedient to His Word. That is why He has given the Spirit to dwell within, giving the ability—the power—to carry out His will. Read Luke 17:7-10 to get a picture of this.

I have a close relative who claims that he is a Christian, but when one looks at his lifestyle, there is a big divide between what he professes and how he lives. He lies and deceives when it's convenient. He's irresponsible with his money, selfish, self-centered, refuses to work, and has little desire to put Christ first.

Basically, we all have one of two spiritual mentors in our lives, and it will be clear which mentor we follow. Either it will be Christ, and our lives reflect Him, or it will be Satan, and our lives will demonstrate this. Where there are lies, deceit, selfishness and no desire to bring any glory to God (but rather to self)—that's surely a lost sinner whose father is Satan.

My relative, even though he professes to others to be a follower of Christ, reflects his true spiritual father, Satan! That's a sad reality to reflect on. I really care and love my relative but it is of critical importance that I wisely discern his true spiritual temperature if I am to minister to his true need. Ignoring the signs would be for me to turn a blind eye to the truth, and my heart aches at this

People may claim to be Christians, but unless they first see themselves as lost, hell-deserving sinners before a God who will hold them accountable for all they do, and come to Him asking for his mercy and salvation through Christ, they have yet to be saved. Only when they come to Him in repentance and faith are they forgiven through Christ's sacrifice on the cross. Only then are they truly born again, regenerated, becoming changed in heart. Only then will they desire to please Christ in all they do show that they are willing to become slaves of Him who bought them from the slave market of sin.

The Real Issue: Jesus as Master

Therefore, prepare your minds for action, keep sober in spirit, fix your hope completely on the grace to be brought to you at the revelation of Jesus Christ. As obedient children, do not be conformed to the former lusts which were yours in your ignorance, but like the Holy One who called you, be holy yourselves also in all your behavior. (1 Peter 1:13-15)

As believers, our view of Lordship is not shaped by our own personal views or wills but instead by the Master who bought us, even with His own blood. We are to be under total submission to our Lord and Master. The terminology of believers being slaves is used over 130 times in the New Testament and is actually a way to true peace and freedom. That's why Jesus said repeatedly:

Then Jesus said to His disciples, "If anyone wishes to come after Me, he must deny himself, and take up his cross and follow Me. For whoever wishes to save his life will lose it; but whoever loses his life for My sake will find it. For what will it profit a man if he gains the whole world and forfeits his soul?"
(Matthew 16:24-26)

When people heard these words of Jesus, and when they heard Him using the terminology of slavery, they knew exactly what He was calling for, so that is why only a few from out of the masses followed Him. What He was saying required a total commitment to Him, a denying of self, giving up of one's rights and options so as to follow a new master instead of following their old, sinful desires.

The ideas of self-esteem and self-worth have crept into the modern church. These all go directly against the biblical view

The Real Issue: Jesus as Master

of a Christian. Those who were once slaves to sin have been bought by a new Master and it is now their desire to do this Master's will. Anyone denying this could easily fall into the hands of the master of darkness, Satan, being ever so deceived by the master-deceiver himself.

But as you think through this, keep in mind that Jesus also warned people by telling them to *"Count the cost."* Every person must realize it's not going to be easy to follow Him, that it will cost them their lives, and they will be a slave to a new master. And what Jesus asks of us actually goes against everything our society tells us concerning self will, self improvement, self determination and striving to be number one. The Bible is really quite emphatic on this point.

If anyone wishes to come after Me, he must deny himself, and take up his cross and follow Me.
(Matthew 16:24)

Every person in every generation makes a choice. And in this process of choosing, there are usually three groups of people. The first of these groups consists of those who, up front, deny Christ and take a hard stance against Him. The second group, which is by far the largest, consists of those who say they believe in Him, read His word once in a while, but in God's view are just as lost as those who reject Him outright. They are not slaves of Christ, but are onlookers from a distance, much like the church in Laodicea in Revelation 3:14-17. Jesus condemns such for being lukewarm. There, the people professing to know Him were religious, but lost; they were hypocrites, professing to know Christ, but not truly belonging to Him. *"But wait,"* you may ask, *"I believe in God and read the Bible."* Just because you believe in God and read the Bible

The Real Issue: Jesus as Master

doesn't make you a slave! Everyone in hell right now believes in God and knows without any doubt that God's word is true. They also have a relationship with God—it's just not a good one. The third group consists of those who are true slaves of Christ. True slaves submit to the will of their master and obey him.

You believe that God is one. You do well; the demons also believe, and shudder. (James 2:19)

As we consider this biblical picture, it is clear that the person who is a prodigal living in outright sin cannot truly be a Christian as defined in Scripture. Prodigals are shouting out in how they live, *"I'm my own master!"* They may have been raised within a Christian context, both at home and in church, but now as adults they have chosen to not follow Him but instead to follow their own desires. John the Apostle witnessed this firsthand. Some may have broken his heart as he saw them become prodigals in the church.

They went out from us, but they were not really of us; for if they had been of us, they would have remained with us; but they went out, so that it would be shown that they all are not of us. (1 John 2:19)

Those who have decided they are their own masters are labeled *"sinners."* This term is used biblically to describe the lost. They habitually walk in sin, and not in righteousness. True believers, even though they sin, too, habitually endeavor with the help of the Holy Spirit to live in obedience to the Word of God, striving toward righteousness. Sinners, being lost, act upon all they have: the flesh. Therefore they speak and act as lost people, and appropriately they are termed prodigals.

The Real Issue: Jesus as Master

In biblical terms, a prodigal is not a Christian. Such a person may be (or may have been) religious but shows no fruit of true repentance or regeneration. In a very real sense, a true Christian should be obvious. True believers love and serve the Lord from a heart of love, compassion and a desire to please Him above all else; they are true slaves to the Master.

But what of the believer who wanders away for a season into a sinful lifestyle? How are we to consider such a person? This kind of situation is the most difficult. It's one thing for a person to deny Christ, walk away from the faith, and declare openly an allegiance to the world and therefore, ultimately, to Satan (John 8:44). It's altogether more puzzling when a person lives in this season of sin and yet still claims to be a Christian; that's difficult to deal with! So what do we do? There are several things.

You should pray, and not only for yourself but for that person. Unfortunately what will probably bring a prodigal back is affliction. God will use this to break into his or her life. Your righteous response should always be predicated on love and compassion with biblical discernment.

> *Brethren, even if anyone is caught in any trespass, you who are spiritual, restore such a one in a spirit of gentleness; each one looking to yourself, so that you too will not be tempted. (Galatians 6:1)*

If times are going well, and if the prodigal's lifestyle is being supported with plenty of money and all the comforts of life are intact, repentance doesn't seem very feasible. There does appear to be a progression that can occur for the believer who takes the path of a sinful lifestyle, and it can be hard to discern if he or she is truly a child of God. However, God may graciously and perfectly orchestrate things in such a way that bad times will come along until there is nothing left but for that person to look up and to demonstrate true reconciliation with God. Sadly, it usually takes this to turn a person around to true repentance. This is also where it may be opportune for the church to come in to help.

If you are a part of a local body of believers who practice accountability of its members and church discipline, you may find that this will have a tremendous impact, not only on the person walking in sin, but on the family of the prodigal. This may be demonstrated in the support of the members through prayer, counsel, guidance, fellowship, love and a team effort to bring the person back into the fold. In cases like this, sometimes the situation may turn out to be a long season, involving the leaders in the church coming alongside to help, and demonstrating the support and concern of the whole local body of Christ.

Let's take a look at this in detail and seek to understand this path of affliction. Specifically, when dealing with people who profess to be believers and yet who who have chosen to walk in sin, there are several things to keep in mind. They are listed below. I've personally developed this approach through experience and cleaving to the biblical principles of love, compassion and discernment.

- **They have usually been warned**: *"But the way of the treacherous is hard"* (Proverbs 13:15). When you talk to them, warn them. So many times people become embarrassed, shy or fearful, and so they don't speak the truth in love to them. But prodigals need to be told the truth as a means to bring about repentance. Be objective, be biblically truthful, but be gracious. I would suggest memorizing Galatians 6:1. Let

your life shine in love so you send a message of winsomeness and attractiveness to them and they know you care.
- **Realize that, as believers, they are grieving the Spirit:** *"And do not grieve the Holy Spirit of God, by whom you were sealed for the day of redemption"* (Ephesians 4:30). The Spirit indwells believers. So, when someone chooses to sin, he or she does so in clear violation of God the Holy Spirit, bringing the emotion of grief to Him. Why? Because He sees everything we do and He knows the consequences of it all. The believer walking daily in habitual sin grieves the indwelling Spirit. So the Spirit will do a work to bring about repentance that will be perfectly fitting for that person in affliction.
- **They go on sinning anyway:** *"Therefore, to one who knows the right thing to do and does not do it, to him it is sin"* (James 4:17). Even though they've been warned and continue to grieve the Spirit, sometimes they continue to walk in habitual sin anyway. It is at this point things will usually turn sour, not only in their conscience but in their daily lives. Perhaps things start falling apart, financially, relationally, emotionally or physically. Sicknesses may occur, relationships may break apart, financial troubles may plague them, or all sorts of life issues may occur. This could possibly be the loving hand of discipline of the Lord.
- **Initiate church discipline** (Matthew 18). If the person is connected to the church in any way (whether a member or not), if you initiate church discipline, this brings spiritual consequences to the situation—for instance, prayer is engaged in and other members who know them call them to repentance. What may happen sometimes, however, is that many people—whether family or friends—try to keep the situation away from the church's knowledge, because of their pride, reputation or a fear of losing a ministry in the

church. The person walking in sin must know he or she will be held accountable not only by God but by the local body of believers who truly care. So, even though some people may give hearty approval for their habitual and sinful behavior, as believers, we are to show our love and care for them, calling them back into the family of God.

- **As time moves on, they may eventually fall again into being a slave to certain sins in their lives** (Romans 6:20-23). This in itself will be a part of God's discipline in their lives. He will use this as a tool of consequence to work upon the believer. An example of this is seen in the life of a friend of mine who made money his idol. God used this to discipline him in such a way that he lost everything—which eventually brought him back in repentance to God.

- **If the person continues to harden his heart toward repentance, he may be delivered over to Satan for the destruction of his flesh** (1 Corinthians 5:5, 11:30). In particular, there are two things to keep in mind here: First, affliction and hard times may well become an instructor to bring him back to God. And, second, this may bring about much prayer on your part, easing your soul somewhat in the realization that God is sovereign and all powerful. If that person is elect, he will surely be saved!

- **Death may occur.** Realize that a person may face the severe discipline of God to the point where God may take his or her life, (1 John 5:16). Why? He has considered the pleasures of this world as more desirable than the great sufferings and resurrection of Christ on our behalf as unworthy. Yes, he may be a believer, but one who has strayed away, and sin now has a stronghold in his life. He has failed to realize that God has given the ability to overcome and escape any sin or temptation, and by his own choice he has walked down a path of affliction.

They went out from us, but they were not really of us; for if they had been of us, they would have remained with us; but they went out, so that it would be shown that they all are not of us. (1 John 2:19)

How much severer punishment do you think he will deserve who has trampled under foot the Son of God, and has regarded as unclean the blood of the covenant by which he was sanctified, and has insulted the Spirit of grace? For we know Him who said, "Vengeance is Mine, I will repay." And again, "The Lord will judge His people." It is a terrifying thing to fall into the hands of the living God. (Hebrews 10:29-31).

There is a sin leading to death. (1 John 5:16)

Postscript

Closing Words to the Hurting

Postscript

Some of the things I've written may appear hard to do, hard to understand, or, maybe for some readers, difficult to put into practice. People grope in bewilderment because of the heartaches associated with dealing with a loved one or friend who has become a prodigal. Our desire for that prodigal is a return to the Lord and a forsaking such trouble due to sin, but sometimes it just doesn't happen. You reason, you share, and you pour out your heart to God, but seemingly to no avail. Tears, torn hearts, and emotional pain are the outcome.

I truly understand, and that's why I have written this book. God's principles have been given to us to guide us through life situations like this, and they can give us both hope and direction. Feelings can be deceptive and misdirecting, leading us to make wrong decisions all the time. And when it comes to dealing with prodigals, our feelings can play such a large role in our decision-making that it has the possibility of causing even more grief. That's why my strong counsel to you is to be obedient to God's principles, no matter how you feel, to cling to Him in your prayers, to delve into God's Word to seek out His principles in making wise decisions and, most importantly, not to isolate yourself from a local body of believers but be connected and active with your local church. Be truth-oriented and not feeling-oriented. Do what is right, for in doing so the fruit will be joy (not necessarily happiness)—biblical joy—as you come to know that God is in complete control.

www.ingramcontent.com/pod-product-compliance
Lightning Source LLC
Chambersburg PA
CBHW070628300426
44113CB00010B/1704